Beyond the Dashboard

From Data Rich to Business Value Through REAL Decisions

LUCY NEMES

Technics Publications
SEDONA, ARIZONA

TECHNICS PUBLICATIONS

115 Linda Vista, Sedona, AZ 86336 USA
https://www.TechnicsPub.com

Edited by Steve Hoberman
Cover design by Lorena Molinari

First Printing 2026

ISBN, print ed. 9798898161361
ISBN, Kindle ed. 9798898161378
ISBN, PDF ed. 9798898161385

Library of Congress Control Number: 2026944826

For Fehmi - my constant, who makes everything possible.

And for Elio, my sunshine - one day you will understand why.

Endorsements

I've built my share of dashboards nobody opened, so Lucy's stories felt like she'd been quietly watching my career and taking notes. She tells it through moments we all recognize and from those she pulls the four patterns that stall data initiatives and the REAL Framework that fixes them. And she doesn't stop at the idea, she hands you the diagnostics, workshops, and templates to act on, which leaves wonderfully little room for excuses to not act. In a world bolting AI onto decisions nobody agreed on, this is the human groundwork that makes it worth having.

Tiankai Feng
Author of "Humanizing Data Strategy" & "Humanizing AI Strategy"

What Patrick Lencioni was to team misalignment, Lucy Nemes is to data dysfunction. If I've said it once, I've said it a thousand times: dashboards are where data goes to die. "Beyond the Dashboard" names that problem precisely and gives you the REAL Framework to fix it. This is the book I wish every client read before their third dashboard refresh.

Jim Sterne, Author, Founder Marketing Analytics Summit

I have always admired Lucy's ability to bring structure to complexity and explain how data can be used to drive better decisions. Reading this book, I frequently found myself smiling, as many of the situations described felt so familiar. You will most likely catch yourself thinking, "This could be my company."

What makes this book stand out is its honest and practical approach. Rather than focusing on theory, Lucy draws on real-life examples to illustrate common challenges and provides concrete tools and guidance to help organizations embed data into decision-making processes early on and turn insights into action. An insightful and highly practical read for anyone looking to close the gap between having data and using it to make better decisions.

Stine Ferse, Director Digital Experience Platform at DHL

Beyond the Dashboard is an insightful and highly practical book for organisations determined to turn data into meaningful business value. Drawing on extensive real-world experience, Lucy Nemes demonstrates that successful data transformation is fundamentally about culture, not technology. The REAL Framework provides a clear, actionable roadmap for embedding data into everyday decisions, strengthening accountability, improving collaboration, and building genuine data confidence across teams. Packed with practical tools, diagnostics, and proven strategies, I strongly believe this book equips leaders, data professionals, and consultants to bridge the gap between insight and action. It is an excellent resource for any organisation seeking lasting, measurable impact from its data investments.

Prashanth Southekal,PhD,MBA,ICD.D
Founder of DBP Institute and D2A2
Adjunct Professor of Decision Intelligence at IE Business School, Spain

Acknowledgments

Writing a book while working as a freelancer and raising a toddler is an exercise in radical prioritization and I could not have done it without the people who quietly, consistently, made space for me to do this.

To my husband, Fehmi: you encouraged me before I had a framework, a book, or a plan. You talked through half-formed ideas more times than either of us can count, and kept things steady when I wasn't sure any of this would come together. Your love and support made this possible.

To my son, Elio: you will probably never remember the weekends spent playing beside my desk, or the mornings when I asked for just five more minutes. You made finishing this feel necessary, and one day, when you're old enough to be curious about what your mom did and why, I hope this book gives you an answer.

To my parents: thank you for supporting a daughter who spent years trying to figure out what she wanted to do. You funded moves across countries and continents, and never once made it feel like a problem. You believed something was coming before I did. And now, you show up again whenever we need you.

To my brother: you flew in when it mattered. You didn't always understand what I was doing or why I kept moving, but you asked, you listened, and you showed up. You still do, whether that means jumping on a plane or coming along so we have an extra pair of hands. That means more than you know.

To my in-laws: thank you for jumping in whenever we needed it. That kind of practical love is what makes everything else possible.

To my dear friends Damjana, Joana, Oliver, and Elin: thank you for celebrating every win with the enthusiasm of people who fully understand what a data strategy consultant does, and even if the details have always been a little fuzzy, the encouragement never was.

On the professional side: Niklas Zillinger, you sat with an early, half-formed version of this framework and gave it serious attention. The conversations we had in those sessions are woven into the bones of the REAL model. This would not exist without that.

Amadeus Tunis, you were the one who convinced me to come back to data and give it another chance. At a moment when I wasn't sure I wanted to, that mattered more than you probably know. André Koriath, you later became my mentor. Together you gave me the freedom to try new things, stayed patient when they didn't work, and never told me what to do when I needed to figure it out myself. That is the difference between a boss and a leader, and I was lucky enough to have two of you.

To the colleagues and clients who gave me room to try things that didn't always work: thank you for the trust, and for staying curious long enough for us to find something that did.

There are also the people who said go at exactly the right moment. Yael Farkas heard me present an early version of this framework at a conference and came up afterward to tell me I had something worth developing. I am genuinely grateful she did. She had no reason to be generous, and she was anyway. And to Tiankai Feng, someone with every reason to ignore a cold message from a stranger, thank you for responding, for offering to talk, and for sharing your experience so openly. Our conversation gave me the confidence to write this book.

Finally, to Steve Hoberman at Technics Publications: thank you for believing in this manuscript before it was fully formed, for saying yes, and for helping shape it into a better book.

Contents

Foreword

I have spent most of my career working with organizations that invested heavily in data, analytics, and AI, only to keep circling the same deceptively simple question: *Why is none of this changing how we actually make decisions?*

It is rarely a problem of technology, information, or talent. Modern companies have the platforms, the dashboards, the models, and a fluent executive vocabulary for being "data-driven." What they lack is the operating muscle to turn that information into action: the cultural readiness to let data into the room when a decision is on the table, and the operational judgment to know how to act on it.

That is why this book matters. I had the privilege of working with Lucy when she was part of my Data, Analytics & AI team at Publicis Sapient. At the time, she was moving back toward the data space with an added CX background that gave her a distinctive advantage: she did not look at analytics as a purely technical discipline. She brought the instincts of customer experience, design thinking, facilitation, and stakeholder empathy into environments that too often treated data as a build problem rather than a behavior-change problem where the real challenge is what happens *after* the dashboard goes live.

That perspective mattered. I had a front-row seat as these ideas took shape, watching Lucy test, adapt, and refine many of the concepts that became the foundation of this book. They came from real client situations: teams that could not agree on a single KPI, dashboards that looked impressive and changed nothing, leaders who wanted insight without knowing what decision the data was meant to support, and data teams frustrated that their work was being used too late, too narrowly, or not at all.

What Lucy understood early is something many organizations still miss: data work is human work. It depends on relationships, clarity, accountability, and confidence. It depends on whether business and data teams are in the room early enough to shape the question; whether someone can say what success looks like before a line of code is written; whether a metric has an owner accountable for what happens when it moves; and whether people have enough fluency to engage with data honestly, especially when the answer is uncomfortable.

The REAL Framework captures this with rare practicality. Relationship, End-goal, Accountability, and Literacy are not abstractions; they are the conditions that decide whether data creates value. They are also precisely the conditions that will determine whether AI becomes a genuine force multiplier or simply accelerates existing dysfunction.

What I admire most is the book's respect for reality. It does not ask you to transform everything before you can improve anything. It offers concrete places to start: better questions, better conversations, better ownership, better rituals. The work is pragmatic, but the implications are significant.

Beyond the Dashboard is a timely, necessary reminder that the value of data lies not in the sophistication of the asset, but in the quality of the decision it enables. For anyone who suspects their organization has more insight than impact, and wants to change that, this book is your field guide.

I am proud to write this foreword, and prouder still to have watched these ideas become an essential framework. This is exactly the kind of practical, human-centered thinking the data and AI field needs more of.

Amadeus Tunis
Data & AI Strategy & Execution Leader
June 2026

Introduction

It was late. After a full day of workshops with a global consumer brand, most of the group had left, and I'd stayed behind for dinner with their senior product lead. We were a glass of wine in when she stopped mid-sentence. "Can I tell you something I didn't say in the room today?" She leaned in. "I know my team built all these dashboards that are supposed to help me prioritize, but I still don't know what to do."

She wasn't criticizing her analysts or complaining about the tools. She was admitting something she hadn't felt safe saying all day: she was surrounded by data and had no idea how to use it to make decisions.

I recognized the feeling immediately. By then, I'd spent over a decade working with data teams, first as an in-house analyst, then as a consultant at a large firm, and then as an independent data strategy expert. I'd built dashboards nobody used and sat through meetings where the numbers changed nothing. Executives were getting weekly reports with dozens of slides and live drill-downs, and yet, when someone had to make an actual decision, like cut a budget, change direction, or kill a feature, the data got cited and then quietly ignored.

A 2024 survey of data leaders found that nearly 80% identified culture, people, and processes as the biggest barriers to becoming data-driven.[1] That matches what I've seen.

When someone senior has already made up their mind, presenting data that contradicts them becomes politically risky, so people protect themselves. They wait to see which way the room is leaning before speaking. They build what you might call KPI theatre - curating metrics that confirm the story already agreed upon in the corridor, not the one the data is actually telling. Dashboards multiply because every team now needs its own set of visuals to defend its budget in the next review. Less truth-seeking, more arms race.

And when the highest-paid opinion enters the room, the room adjusts. Not to the data, but to the temperature.

The result is predictable: more dashboards, more reports, more motion, but no change in how decisions get made.

Most organizations respond the same way: by adopting another platform, offering training, or implementing a transformation program. More activity, but little progress. And each time, the underlying patterns stay exactly where they are.

---

[1] **2024 Wavestone Data & AI Leadership Executive Survey:** 77.6% of surveyed executives cite culture/people/process/organization as the principal challenge to becoming data-driven (not tech limitations).

Over time, I noticed that the dysfunction took the same shape regardless of industry or company size. Data teams got involved too late to influence decisions. The goals remained vague enough that no one could clearly define success or failure. Ownership was diffused across functions, so no one acted when metrics moved. And people lacked the confidence to challenge assumptions in front of senior stakeholders, so decisions got made the same way they always had. Four patterns. Different industries, companies, and leadership teams, but the same four patterns underneath. Not because the data was wrong, but because using it honestly carried a cost most people weren't willing to pay.

I started experimenting with ways to change those patterns. Some approaches failed quietly, others expensively. But a smaller set of changes consistently worked: involving data earlier, clarifying decisions before building dashboards, making ownership explicit, and building confidence rather than compliance. When those shifts happened, data stopped decorating decisions and started shaping them.

That's the REAL Framework: Relationship, End-goal, Accountability, and Literacy. It's the foundation of this book.

This isn't a manifesto about becoming "data-driven". Most companies already think they are. It's a practical book about how decisions get made inside organizations, and why data so often fails to influence them.

When the REAL Framework takes hold, something changes in the room. Teams stop arguing about numbers and start deciding what to do with them.

Part I breaks down the patterns that stall data initiatives. Part II introduces the REAL Framework and the behavioral shifts behind it. The Field Guide provides practical tools, workshops, and diagnostics to apply within your own organization.

The stories in this book are based on real client situations. Identifying details have been changed and, in some cases, combined to protect confidentiality.

Data doesn't create value on its own; decisions do. And culture determines whether data ever gets the chance to shape them.

PART I

Data Without Decisions

Most organizations don't have a data problem. They have a decision problem.

Despite unprecedented investment in dashboards, analytics platforms, AI, and data teams, many organizations still make important decisions the same way they always have: through hierarchy, intuition, and habit. Data is present, but it rarely changes the outcome.

This part explores why. Through real examples and recurring organizational patterns, you'll see how data becomes disconnected from decision-making long before anyone notices. Rather than treating these as isolated failures, you'll learn to recognize the four underlying patterns that quietly undermine even the strongest analytics capabilities.

Once you can see these patterns, they become difficult to ignore. More importantly, they become possible to change.

Chapter 1

Why Data Initiatives Stall

Every company has a dashboard graveyard; you just can't see it.

It doesn't exist in a single location you can visit. It's distributed across BI tools, shared drives, PowerPoint presentations, and bookmarked browser tabs collecting dust. Dozens of dashboards, sometimes hundreds, built with good intentions and optimism but quietly ignored by everyone who asked for them.

Here's how it usually happens: First, a business team asks for visibility into something. Then an analyst sees an opportunity to help, so they gather requirements and consult the stakeholders. They review the mockups, align (at least it feels like an alignment), and finally, a dashboard goes live. A link to the dashboard gets shared in Slack or Teams, and someone says "looks good", and then nothing. No follow-up questions, no decisions, no change in behavior. The dashboard exists and is updated regularly, and matters to precisely no one.

What's actually happening

Most dashboards don't fail because they're poorly designed or built on the wrong platform. They fail because they were never connected to an actual question in the first place. The data is present but peripheral. It shows up in the presentations to validate choices that were already made; it is cited when it helps, and it is challenged when it doesn't.

This is data-decorated decision-making. The decision comes first, and the data just tags along to make it look rational. Under pressure, people rarely search for the truth. They search for confirmation.[2]

I watched this play out at a consumer-packaged goods (CPG) client in 2023 that was deciding whether to expand into a new geographic market. The executive team had already decided to expand, based largely on the CEO's conviction that "This is our moment." The strategy team (where I got involved) was asked to build a "data-driven case" to support the move. The final presentation included data analysis, customer research, and financial modeling. It all pointed in one direction: expand. What the presentation didn't include was the analysis that showed customer acquisition costs in that market were three times higher

---

[2] Daniel Kahneman, *Thinking, Fast and Slow* (Farrar, Straus and Giroux, 2011). Kahneman distinguishes between System 1 thinking, which is fast, intuitive, and prone to cognitive bias, and System 2 thinking, which is slower and more deliberate. In high-pressure decision environments, System 1 dominates, and data that contradicts an existing conviction tends to get filtered out rather than processed.

than in their established regions, nor that two competitors had tried the same expansion and quietly retreated within 18 months. That analysis existed; it was identified, discussed, and ultimately dismissed because it didn't fit the story the CEO wanted. The decision had already been made before the data entered the room.

I saw this pattern again at another retail client with multiple dashboards measuring "conversion." One dashboard defined it as completed purchases, another as add-to-cart rate, a third focused on checkout starts, and a fourth defined conversion as sessions where users added at least one item to cart. Nothing was technically wrong: the data was accurate, and the dashboards were polished. However, each dashboard was reviewed by a different group and had a slightly different context, yet the metrics still showed up in decks under "conversion". The product team, the marketing team, and the regional managers each had their preferred dashboard, and they spent hours in meetings arguing about which definition and whose numbers were "right." Meanwhile, the actual business suffered because delivery issues went unresolved. Customer complaints increased by 18%, and NPS fell by 7 score points in a single quarter. The dashboards were beautiful, frequently referenced and discussed, yet completely beside the point.

Here's what "data-driven" has become in most companies: dashboards are presented as proof that the company is sophisticated. They signal modernity and control. Executives mention them in all-hands meetings, recruiters highlight them in job postings, and consultants admire them in deck reviews.

However, when they are making decisions, budgets still follow gut instinct and are non-negotiably defined one year in advance before any signal even exists. Product roadmaps still chase the loudest executive's opinion, and marketing spend still goes to the agency that makes the most compelling case in the room without any ROI estimates. Dashboards get checked after decisions are made, not before. They're used to justify choices that were already locked in, not to inform what those choices should be.

"We have five dashboards and I still don't know what to do."

I've heard variations of this complaint from marketers, product managers, executives, and frustrated analysts at various companies over the past years.

Marketing manager lead at a CPG company: "We have the Customer engagement dashboard, the User activity report, the Digital touchpoint tracker, the Platform usage metrics, and the Interaction analytics view, all measuring basically the same thing, but I still don't know which channel to invest in."

CFO of a scale-up: "I don't trust the data enough to take it to the board."

CEO of a fashion retail start-up: "I don't know if we're getting value from this team. Do we even need them?"

These aren't complaints about data quality, the data team, or the quality of their work. They're expressing confusion about what to do with all this information.

The gap isn't between what people have and what they want. It's between data availability and data usefulness. It's between seeing numbers and knowing what they mean, and between having dashboards and making decisions.

My first contribution to the dashboards graveyard

The first dashboard I built that nobody used still bothers me 15 years later.

I was fresh out of university, newly hired, and eager to prove myself. I was full of SQL skills and confidence. I understood the product and the business model and built what I genuinely believed was a useful dashboard for the product team. It had everything: clean design, relevant metrics and filters, smart segmentation. When I presented it, the team nodded, and the main product owner even said, "Great work", and I was so proud. The meeting moved on, but nobody asked a single follow-up question. A week later, I checked the usage logs: three views - two were mine, and one was probably someone clicking the link by accident.

The dashboard was technically perfect and functionally useless.

At first, I blamed them for not using it. Then I thought they probably don't understand it, so I blamed myself for making it too complicated. After building many more dashboards, all with a similar fate, I got curious about why this kept happening, not just to me, but to virtually every analyst I knew. Because here's the pattern I was and still am noticing:

Tools keep improving and dashboards get more sophisticated. Companies spend hundreds of thousands on Snowflake, Databricks, Tableau, Power BI....
They hire dozens of data scientists and analysts, but decisions are still made the same way they always have.

What this costs you

Unused dashboards are usually framed as wasted analyst time. That's true, but it's the smallest part of the problem. The real cost is trust.

Every dashboard that gets built and ignored teaches the company something dangerous: data is optional. Analytics is a service you request when you need a chart for a deck, not a partner in making better decisions. Delivering the insight is the end of the job, what happens after isn't the data team's problem.

This erodes confidence on both sides. Business teams stop expecting data to help and data teams stop believing their work will make a difference. The result is a mutual disengagement, hidden under more dashboards, more tools, and more meetings.

But there's an even higher cost: opportunity cost. At that retail company with several "conversion" dashboards, they missed an entire quarter where they could have been fixing their fulfillment process. Instead, they argued about methodology. At the CPG company expanding into a new market, the first year of investment was largely wasted because the data that could have prevented the decision never made it past the CEO's conviction. At another tech startup, they kept building features nobody wanted because their product analytics showed usage was growing, but they never looked at which feature the users who stayed were actually using. It was a completely different one.

The real cost of dashboard graveyards isn't analysts' time, it's the decisions that could have been better but weren't. The worst part is that most companies don't even realize it's happening.

What it feels like on the inside

Nobody is explicitly anti-data, and most people genuinely want to use it. But engaging with data starts to feel slow, risky, and uncomfortable, especially under pressure when someone senior is waiting for an answer.

Business teams are told to be "data-driven" but rarely told which metrics matter right now, what question a specific dashboard is supposed to answer, or what to do when the data is inconclusive. Definitions shift just enough to create doubt. Context is always partial. So naturally they protect themselves: waiting for someone senior to speak first, cherry-picking the metric that supports the argument they already wanted to make, or defaulting to experience because that doesn't need defense. Data stops being a tool for better thinking. It becomes exposure - another way to be wrong in front of your peers.

Inside **data teams**, the dynamic is different but just as corrosive. Requests arrive after the strategy is locked. Priorities change mid-flight. Context is missing. So teams optimize for delivery: build the dashboard, close the ticket, move on. Speed becomes the proxy for success because impact is too hard to measure and too politically fraught to claim.

The clearest signal of this dysfunction shows up in meetings. Someone shares a dashboard and walks through the numbers. Attendees listen and nod thoughtfully. Then someone, usually someone senior, says: "Based on my experience..." or "My gut tells me..." or "I think what we're really seeing here is...", and the decision gets made exactly the way it would have without any data at all. The data was present; it just didn't participate.

The predictable response that makes things worse

When companies realize their "dashboards aren't working", the instinct is always the same: add more. More metrics, granularity, drill-downs, real-time data, governance frameworks, AI features that promise to surface insights automatically, training sessions on how to use the tools, and data literacy programs. Adding technology to a broken system doesn't fix the system; it just makes the dysfunction more expensive.[3] The problem isn't the tools. It's everything around them.

I watched a financial services company respond to low dashboard adoption by launching a "Data Days" training series. They taught 200 people how to use Tableau over six weeks in mandatory training. People learned how to create calculated fields and build dual-axis charts. Three months later, dashboard usage was exactly where it started, because the problem wasn't that people didn't know how to use Tableau. The problem was that they didn't know what decisions the dashboards were supposed to help them make.

---

[3] For more on why technology investment without organizational redesign consistently underdelivers, see Jeanne Ross, Cynthia Beath & Martin Mocker, Designed for Digital: How to Architect Your Business for Sustained Success (MIT Press, 2019).

At a logistics company I worked with, one of the product teams had a dashboard with 33 metrics. When I asked which ones influenced decisions, the VP of customer experience stared at the screen for a moment and said, "Honestly? We look at the number of leads generated, customer satisfaction, and the number of complaints. The rest is just there." 30 metrics that existed but didn't matter. They were built, maintained, refreshed, yet completely ignored by the team.

When everything is supposedly important, nothing is.

People stop engaging not because they're lazy or resistant to data. They stop because the signal-to-noise ratio is unbearable. Data becomes something you check out of obligation, not something you use to think better.

The problem isn't that people lack information; they're drowning in it. What they lack is clarity about what matters, ownership over what happens next, and enough confidence to trust data when it contradicts their instincts. Adding more complexity to a system that's already overwhelming doesn't make it work better; it just creates the illusion of progress while the fundamental dysfunction persists.

Why good dashboards still fail

Here's the part that's hardest to accept, especially if you're an analyst who's poured hours into building something thoughtful: Most unused dashboards are technically fine. The data is accurate, the visualizations are clear, the refresh schedule works, and the performance is good. By every objective measure of dashboard quality, they should work. They fail because they were built in isolation from the question or decisions they're supposed to support.

I see this pattern everywhere: dashboards designed around all available metrics rather than actual questions. They show everything, but they prioritize nothing. There is no clear owner for what happens when a certain number moves, no shared understanding of what "good" looks like, let alone what to do when you're not hitting it. In other words, the dashboard exists, just the decision system around it doesn't.

And here's what almost no one wants to acknowledge: the dysfunction isn't random, it's structural. The same patterns show up again and again across different industries, company sizes, and levels of technical sophistication.

The problem is not dashboard quality; it is the decision system around the dashboard: no owner, no shared definition of success, no moment where the data is allowed to change the plan. Once you see that, the pattern becomes hard to miss. It shows up in four forms. That is where we go next.

CHAPTER 2

The Four Failure Patterns

Data initiatives rarely fail in one dramatic moment. They stall through habits: predictable patterns of working that quietly neutralize data regardless of how sophisticated your tools are or how talented your team is.

I've seen these patterns in retail, tech, CPG, financial services, logistics, and automotive. Different industries and company sizes, different org structures, different levels of data maturity, but the same four failure modes:

- **Organizational misalignment**: Data teams and business teams operate on parallel tracks, with data delivered too late to inform decisions.
- **Strategic ambiguity**: Goals are vague enough that no metric can definitively indicate success or failure, leading to dashboards that answer no clear question.

- **Operational gaps**: Responsibility for acting on data is so diffused that nobody owns what happens when numbers move.
- **Cultural lag**: People lack the confidence to interpret data, challenge it appropriately, or admit confusion, so they retreat to instinct.

These patterns don't exist in isolation. They compound, creating a cycle that makes data matter less and less in how work gets done. Here's how to recognize each one, and what they cost you.

Pattern 1: Organizational misalignment

This is the failure pattern that feels most organizational: siloed teams, low trust between functions, and late engagement of data in decision processes.

How it shows up

In most companies, data teams and business teams operate on parallel tracks that occasionally intersect but never truly converge. Data gets brought in at the end to validate a choice, explain what happened, and produce a report for the board. Not at the beginning, where it might shape direction or challenge assumptions.

By the time dashboards appear, goals are already locked, budgets are already allocated, and opinions are already hardened into positions people will defend. At that point, data can only react to decisions rather than inform them. It can describe what happened but not influence what happens next.

What it looks like in practice

At an automotive company I worked with in 2021, the marketing team planned its annual campaign strategy in September. They set objectives, allocated budget across channels, and designed creative concepts. In November, two months later, they asked the data team to build dashboards to "track performance." Not to help shape the strategy, or to test assumptions about channel and message effectiveness. Just to track what was already decided.

When I asked the analytics lead why they weren't involved earlier, she laughed. "They don't think to include us until execution. By then, it's too late to influence anything meaningful."

The campaigns launched in January. By March, it was clear that two of the five channels were underperforming badly, acquisition costs were 40% higher than projected, and customer quality was significantly lower. The data showed this clearly. But changing course would mean admitting the strategy was flawed. It also meant reallocating budget mid-year and explaining to leadership why the original plan wasn't working. So, they didn't. They rode it out and spent the full budget. They didn't hit any of their targets and blamed the "market conditions."

Why it persists

This pattern persists because it's comfortable. Business teams don't have to validate their plans with data early when the evidence might contradict what they want to do. Data teams don't have to engage in messy strategic debates where the answer isn't in a dataset, and don't have to leave their comfort zone. Both sides avoid conflict and stay in their lanes. The cost is that data never influences anything that matters.

The consequences

This situation creates tension on both sides. Business teams feel unsupported because the data team is never there when they need them, and they don't understand their challenges. Data teams feel used because they're seen just as the dashboard factory and because nobody listens to their recommendations.

Without early collaboration built into how work flows, data becomes transactional instead of strategic. And transactions don't change behavior; they just document it.

Pattern 2: Strategic ambiguity

This pattern is more insidious because it often masquerades as flexibility or agility.

How it shows up

Many dashboards fail because they answer the wrong question. Or worse, they answer no question at all. They exist because someone thought visibility would be valuable and interesting, but nobody articulated what decision that visibility should enable.

Teams track dozens of metrics but struggle to articulate what success looks like beyond vague aspirations like "improve customer experience" or "drive growth". They can't clearly state which decisions matter most right now or what trade-offs they're willing to make when goals conflict.

What it looks like in practice

A hospitality technology company I consulted for in 2018 had a product team tracking 47 different metrics for its core platform. When I asked the product lead what success would look like in the next quarter, he said, "We want to improve engagement and reduce churn." I pushed: "If you could only move three metrics, which three would prove you'd succeeded?" Long pause. "That's a good question."

We tried to answer it, but the team couldn't agree. Engineering cared about technical performance metrics, product cared about feature adoption, customer success cared about support ticket volume, and marketing cared about activation rates. Everyone had their preferred definition of "success," but they didn't align, so they tracked everything. This also meant that they didn't prioritize anything. When engagement dropped 6% but churn improved slightly and feature adoption stayed flat, nobody knew if that was good or bad. Conversations became debates over methodology rather than decisions about action. Three months later, they were still debating what the metrics meant; there were no strategic pivots, no resource reallocation, and no change in approach.

Why it persists

Strategic ambiguity persists because clarity is hard.

It requires making choices about what matters most, which means admitting some things matter less. It requires aligning stakeholders with different priorities and having leaders commit to specific outcomes they can be held accountable for.

Vagueness is much safer. If your goal is "improve customer experience", you can always find a metric that shows progress. If your goal is "increase 30-day retention from 62% to 68% by reallocating onboarding resources from content to human touchpoints", you're either right or wrong, and being provably wrong is uncomfortable.

The consequences

Without clear end goals, dashboards become collections of interesting information rather than decision-support tools. Activity replaces impact, visibility replaces direction, and so people see the data but don't know what to do with it.

This is why companies end up with 47 metrics on a dashboard when they only need five. Nobody wanted to make the hard call about what matters most, so everything made the cut. And when everything is tracked, nothing is prioritized.

Pattern 3: Operational gaps

Even when goals are reasonably clear and teams are reasonably aligned, execution breaks down at the operational level.

How it shows up

Dashboards get shared widely, everyone has access, transparency is high, but responsibility is completely diffused. If a KPI moves unexpectedly, nobody can clearly answer: "Who explains why?" "Who decides what happens next?" "Who is accountable for whether things improve?" In many companies, the answer is "The team" or "We all are," which functionally means nobody.

What it looks like in practice

At a retail company I worked with in 2020, they had a beautiful "Store Performance Dashboard" that every regional manager could access. It showed sales, foot traffic, conversion rates, average basket size, and inventory turnover, all updated daily.

Customer satisfaction scores started declining in one region. Not dramatically, just a slow, steady drop from 6.2 to 5.9 on a ten-point scale over eight weeks. Everyone could see it, and it was even discussed in different weekly meetings. I asked the regional VP: "Who owns fixing this?" "The store managers," he said. I asked the store managers, and they said, "Regional operations set the policies we follow." I asked regional operations, and they said, "We provide the framework, but execution is up to store managers."

Classic diffusion. Everyone could see the problem, yet nobody owned the solution. The satisfaction score kept dropping, and by the time they finally acted, twelve weeks in, they'd lost meaningful market share to a competitor, and recovery took six months.

Why it persists

Diffused ownership persists because it protects people from accountability.

If nobody owns a metric, nobody can be blamed when it goes wrong. This is particularly common with "shared" metrics that cross functional boundaries.

There's also the incentive problem: data teams often get measured on delivery speed and stakeholder satisfaction, not on whether their work changed outcomes. Business teams get measured on hitting targets, not on whether they used data to get there. So, everyone has their own metrics, and using data well falls into the gap between them.

The consequences

Without clear ownership, metrics don't trigger action, insights don't turn into decisions, and performance discussions stay safely theoretical. Everyone can see the retention rate dropped 5% but nobody's job depends on fixing it, so it gets discussed and then nothing. Transparency without accountability creates noise, not momentum. It's like having a fire alarm that everyone can hear but nobody is responsible for responding to. Eventually, people learn to ignore it.

Pattern 4: Cultural lag

This is the failure pattern that's least visible on org charts and often most damaging in practice.

How it shows up

Most people no longer lack access to data; most companies solved that problem years ago. What they lack is confidence using it: they're unsure how to interpret numbers, how to challenge them appropriately, how to talk about uncertainty in front of senior leaders, or how to admit they don't understand something without looking incompetent. So, they hedge and defer to whoever sounds most confident, or default to intuition, not because intuition is better, but because it feels safer. You can't be proven wrong about a gut feeling the way you can be wrong about a data interpretation.

What it looks like in practice

I facilitated a quarterly business review at a logistics company in 2023. The analytics team presented a detailed analysis showing that their premium delivery tier was unprofitable in 40% of their markets: customer acquisition costs were too high, margins were too thin, and volume wasn't sufficient to justify the dedicated infrastructure. The recommendation was clear: exit those markets, reallocate resources to the profitable ones, and focus on the segments where the unit economics worked. The room went quiet until the SVP of operations spoke: "I hear what the data is saying, but my experience tells me we need to be in those markets for brand presence. If we pull out, we'll lose credibility."

Nobody pushed back. Not the CFO, who'd been complaining about margin pressure for months, nor the CEO, who'd been asking for cost optimization. Not even the head of strategy, who'd commissioned the analysis. Later, I asked the analytics lead why she didn't challenge the SVP's "experience" when her data clearly contradicted it. "I'm not going to tell him he's wrong in front of the CEO. If he wants to ignore the analysis, that's his choice."

The company stayed in those markets and lost an estimated €3.2M over the next fiscal year. Eventually, they exited anyway, but only after the financial impact became undeniable.

Why it persists

Cultural lag persists because companies reward certainty over curiosity. Admitting you don't understand something feels like weakness, and questioning a senior leader's intuition feels like insubordination. When people do not feel safe speaking candidly, asking difficult questions, or challenging authority, many choose caution instead. They wait, they defer, and they protect themselves.[4]

There's also the storytelling gap. Data teams often present findings as if the numbers speak for themselves, but they don't. Numbers need context, narrative, and connection to decisions people care about. When that translation doesn't happen, data feels technical, abstract, and irrelevant, even when it's directly related to someone's goals.

And then there's tool overload. Companies pile on platforms: one BI tool, another for data science, another for marketing analytics, yet another for operational reporting, and expect people to develop fluency across all of them while also doing their actual jobs. The cognitive overhead becomes unbearable.

The consequences

When confidence is low, engagement drops. And when engagement drops, dashboards get ignored, and the company

---

[4] For more on how the absence of psychological safety shapes behavior in teams and organizations, see Amy C. Edmondson, *The Fearless Organization: Creating Psychological Safety in the Workplace for Learning, Innovation, and Growth* (Wiley, 2018).

concludes: "Data doesn't work here." Which becomes a self-fulfilling prophecy.

People retreat to what feels safe: experience, hierarchy, consensus. Data becomes optional, something you reference if it supports your position, something you question if it doesn't.

How the patterns reinforce each other

These four patterns don't exist in isolation; they feed each other.

When data teams join late, they can't help define what success looks like. This makes ownership impossible because nobody wants to own a goal they can't define or numbers they don't understand. And when ownership is fuzzy, people lose confidence in using data because if it goes wrong, they might get blamed.

At the automotive company from Pattern 1, I watched this play out in real time. The data team wasn't involved in strategy (Pattern 1), so no clear success metrics were defined for the campaign (Pattern 2). When performance lagged, no one owned the decision to pivot (Pattern 3). And the marketing team lacked the confidence to challenge the original strategy, even when the data was clear (Pattern 4).

Result: a failed campaign, millions wasted, and a data team that became even more marginalized in the next planning cycle. No dashboard can fix that, and no amount of training on Tableau will address it. AI models can't compensate for that either. This is why companies can pour millions into data infrastructure and still feel completely stuck. They're solving technical problems while ignoring the cultural ones that determine whether data gets used.

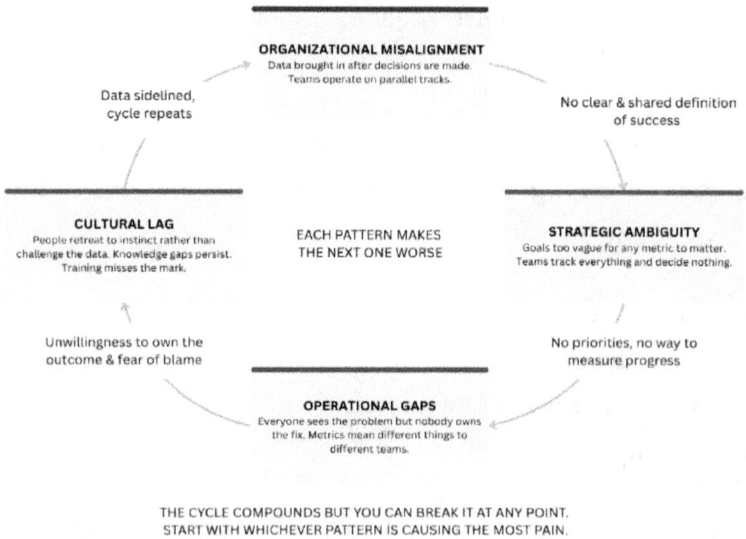

Figure 1: The four failure patterns don't exist in isolation; they compound. Each one makes the next harder to solve. But the cycle can be broken at any point. That's what the REAL Framework is for.

What comes next

The good news is that each of these failure patterns has a clear countermove in the form of a deliberate change in how teams work with data. This is what the REAL Framework is.

Organizational misalignment is countered by **Relationship**; building genuine partnership between data and business teams, with data embedded early in decision processes.

Strategic ambiguity is countered by **End-goal**; defining clear, specific decisions that data needs to support, with concrete criteria for success.

Operational gaps are countered by **Accountability**; making ownership explicit, so everyone knows who's responsible when metrics move.

Cultural lag is countered by **Literacy**; building confidence through shared language, storytelling that connects data to decisions, and psychological safety to engage honestly with uncertainty.

Together, these four countermoves form the REAL Framework: **Relationship, end-goal, accountability, literacy**. That's what Part II is about. Not as abstract principles, but as concrete practices you can start using Monday morning.

Because once you fix the culture, once you create the conditions where data can be useful, the dashboards you already have suddenly start to matter.

PART II

The Fix - REAL Framework

If Part I explains why data initiatives stall, Part II shows how to change the conditions that allow them to succeed.

The REAL Framework was developed through years of practical work with organizations facing the same recurring challenges. It is built around four pillars: Relationship, End-goal, Accountability, and Literacy. Together, they address the cultural and organizational barriers that prevent data from influencing decisions.

Each chapter introduces one pillar, explains why it matters, and provides practical approaches you can apply without waiting for a major transformation program. The goal isn't to create more process. It's to change how decisions are made, one conversation, one project, and one team at a time.

Chapter 3

From Diagnosis to Fix

The first time I presented these ideas publicly, I was nervous. I had been testing pieces of the framework with clients and refining the language, but I hadn't stood in front of a room full of strangers and said, "This is what is broken, and this is how to fix it."

What I wasn't prepared for was the nodding. Not polite nodding, but the kind that happens when people recognize something they've felt but never quite named. After the session, people came up and said variations of the same thing: "This is exactly what's happening in our company. You need to do something with this."

By now, if Part I did its job, you probably had a similar moment somewhere in those paragraphs. Not recognition of something new, but recognition of something you already knew and hadn't quite named. You've seen how dashboards accumulate while decisions stay stubbornly unchanged, how teams talk about being data-informed yet revert to instinct the moment pressure rises.

This happens because data is rarely set up to participate in decisions when it matters. So, what changes how data shows up in decisions?

Most organizations respond by adding more: another tool or a model, a program or an outside consultancy to fix it and make it stick. These efforts are well-intentioned, but often ineffective. They describe what good should look like, but they rarely change how work unfolds on an ordinary working day.

The REAL Framework exists for a different purpose.

What is REAL?

REAL is not a maturity model or a transformation program. It is a way to change the conditions under which data gets used. REAL grew out of practice, not from theory. It came from watching the same four things break across enough companies and industries that the pattern became impossible to ignore: late involvement, vague goals, diffused ownership, and low confidence. Each of these breaks now has a pillar: Relationship, End-goal, Accountability, Literacy.

The four pillars aren't sequential steps you complete in order, and they're not a hierarchy where mastering one unlocks the next. They're four parallel levers, and you can pull any one of them independently.

Most companies need to work on all four, but they should start with whichever one is causing the most pain or is expected to have the biggest return. If you'd rather not guess, the REAL Diagnostic in the Field Guide will tell you where to start. It takes 16 questions and about 10 minutes, and gives you a direct route to the chapter that matters most for your situation.

Each pillar is a direct response to one of the failure patterns from Part I:

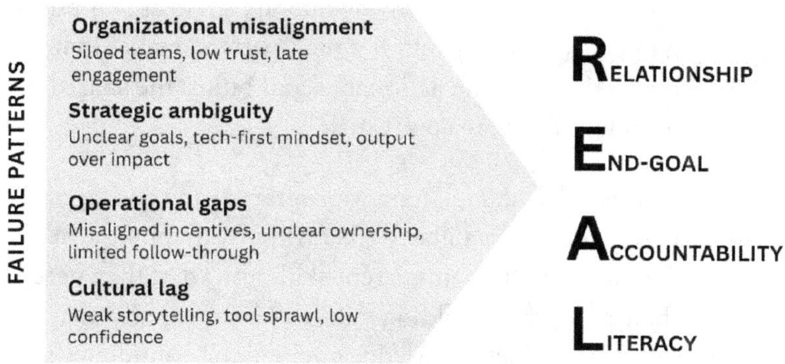

Figure 2: The REAL Framework mapped against the four failure patterns. Each pillar is a direct response to one specific way data initiatives stall.

If something in Part I made you think "that's us," the chapter you need is probably already obvious. Here's what each one is:

- **Relationship**: Most data teams are brought in after important decisions have been made, and in the meantime, they are treated like a help desk. This pillar is about changing that by embedding data in the work of the business early enough that it can shape direction, not just report on it.

- **End-goal**: Most analyses start with the data and work forward to whatever it shows. This pillar reverses that by starting with the decision that needs to be made, and working backward to only the data that matters. That means helping stakeholders figure out what question they're trying to answer, and making sure the final output is designed around what someone needs to *do* with it, not just what's available to show.

- **Accountability**: Most metrics have owners on paper but not really in practice. When something is everyone's responsibility, it's effectively nobody's. This pillar puts a name next to every number that matters, makes that ownership real and actionable, and builds the shared foundation that makes it stick.

- **Literacy**: Most data literacy programs run training and call it a day. This pillar starts earlier by mapping where people are with their current skills and what they need in their roles, then building tailored learning paths that develop not just knowledge but genuine confidence to engage with data when it matters, with the conditions to scale that across the organization over time.

Start with the pillar that's most broken - there's no executive mandate to wait for, no reorganization to plan. Change happens through small moves: a planning meeting, a dashboard request, a metric review, an uncomfortable decision. But small moves compound. When they do, dashboards stop being decorative, not because they change, but because the system around them does.

AI impact

Every conversation I have with clients these days contains a version of the same question, and it usually comes after I've described the REAL Framework, and after someone has recognized their organization in the failure patterns. And then: "But doesn't AI change all of this?"

It's a fair question, because the tools available to teams in 2026 are genuinely different from what existed five years ago. Copilot surfaces anomalies before anyone thinks to look for them; language models write the first draft of the analysis; and automated pipelines flag when a metric moves outside expected ranges and generate a plain-English explanation of why. If the old problem was that insight was hard to produce, and now insight is cheap, fast, and available on demand, that makes the cultural problems even more urgent.

Every failure pattern from Part I can get worse with AI.

More insight surfaced faster, but into an organization that hasn't agreed on what decisions it's trying to make; that's not progress. That's more noise at higher volume.

Think about what each failure pattern looks like when you add AI to it:

- **Organizational misalignment** means the data team is handed a request to support a direction they had no part in shaping. AI makes the deck faster to produce but it doesn't change when data entered the room, or the fact that the analysis was always going to decorate a decision rather than shape it.

- **Strategic ambiguity** means nobody has agreed on what question they're trying to answer. AI will answer any question you give it fluently and confidently, which is precisely the problem. Vague questions now get authoritative-sounding responses, and the gap between what was asked and what needed deciding becomes even harder to spot.

- **Operational gaps** mean the metric has a name but no owner, and no one is doing anything about it. AI can now tell you the metric is declining, diagnose the likely cause, and suggest interventions. It still can't tell you who is responsible for acting on it, or make sure they actually do.

- **Cultural lag** means people don't have the skills or confidence to know what to do with data in the first place. AI-generated insights don't close that gap; they widen it. When the analysis arrives pre-packaged, there's even less reason to develop the muscle, and even less ability to spot when the output is wrong.

The deeper issue is that AI optimizes for the step you give it. Give it a clear question, a named decision, a defined owner, and a team confident enough to pressure-test the output, and it's a genuine force multiplier. Give it the mess that most organizations have, and it produces more sophisticated-looking versions of the same mess. And it will do so confidently, because AI will never tell you your question doesn't make sense, flag that it might be wrong, or admit when it's filling gaps with fiction. The burden of knowing what to ask and whether to trust the answer falls entirely on the humans in the room.

AI is extraordinarily good at turning signal into insight. What it can't do is turn insight into action. That gap, between insight and action, analysis and decision, and knowing and doing, is exactly where the REAL Framework operates. Not as a competitor to AI, but as the foundation that determines whether AI produces anything useful at all.

The organizations that will get the most out of AI are those where data teams are embedded early enough that the right questions are asked before anyone touches a tool. Where every output connects to a decision for which someone is accountable. Where people are confident enough to challenge the model when something looks wrong. In other words, the ones that have done the cultural work first.

REAL isn't the alternative to AI.
It's what makes AI worth having.

How to read this part

Each of the next four chapters goes deep on one pillar: the failure pattern it addresses, the levers available to you, what good looks like in practice, and what it takes to make progress in an organization that isn't starting from zero.

You can read Part II straight through or skip directly to the chapter that matches your most urgent problem right now. The pillars are independent enough that pulling one lever from End-goal and one from Accountability, while leaving the rest for later, is a completely legitimate way to work. Most change efforts look exactly like that: partial, pragmatic, and shaped by what's possible right now. Still, each pillar addresses a different reason why data fails to influence decisions, and the fuller picture only emerges when you've seen all four. If you have the time, read it straight through. You'll likely recognize something in every chapter.

CHAPTER 4

Relationship

At some point, almost every data team becomes a help desk. Nobody announces it or decides it; it just happens. It usually looks like this: a request comes in, phrased reasonably. "Can you build a dashboard tracking campaign performance? We need it by Friday." The data team reads it, maybe asks a few clarifying questions, and gets to work. By Friday, the report is done, and someone replies with "Great, thanks", and by the following Thursday, nobody's looked at it.

This is the ticket-in, report-out dynamic. A request comes in, an output goes out, and somewhere between those two events, any possibility of actual influence quietly disappears. The analyst did exactly what she was asked and the business team got exactly what they requested. Yet, both sides end up frustrated - the data team because their work isn't being used, and the business team because the report isn't telling them what to do. Meanwhile, a decision is made on gut feel that data could have shaped if the setup were different.

The reason is simple. By the time a ticket arrives, the important decisions have already happened. Someone decided what the campaign was trying to achieve, set the budget, and defined the audience and the success criteria. Those decisions shaped which questions are worth asking, which metrics should matter, and what the data would need to show to change anyone's behavior. The data team wasn't in any of those conversations; they were brought in at execution and asked to build something that would report on a plan they'd had no part in making.

Here's the part that's hardest to admit: most data teams know this isn't working. Ask any analyst privately whether "number of tickets closed" tells you anything meaningful about their team's impact, and they'll tell you no. Closing 50 tickets whose outputs never influenced a single decision is worse than closing five that did, and they know that. And yet those are the metrics data teams use to report their own success: tickets closed, reports delivered, requests completed on time. Not because anyone believes these numbers reflect real value, but because they're the only numbers available when you're never close enough to decisions to measure anything more meaningful. You can't track influence on outcomes you weren't part of shaping. So, the team adapts, optimizes for what it can control, and over time, the metric stops being a proxy for something and just becomes the KPI. The report factory runs efficiently, and nobody questions whether it should exist.

This is what organizational misalignment looks like in practice: not conflict, not deliberate exclusion, just a structural default that keeps data at the edge of the decision.[5]

The R in REAL stands for Relationship. It is the countermove to organizational misalignment, and it's about building structural partnerships and changing how and when data teams show up in the work of the business: not reacting to it, not servicing it, but being part of it from the beginning, when decisions are still open. Three levers make that shift possible. **Early presence** gets data into the room when work starts, **common ground** makes sure that conversation leads somewhere, and **Stakeholder landscape** keeps the right people invested throughout.

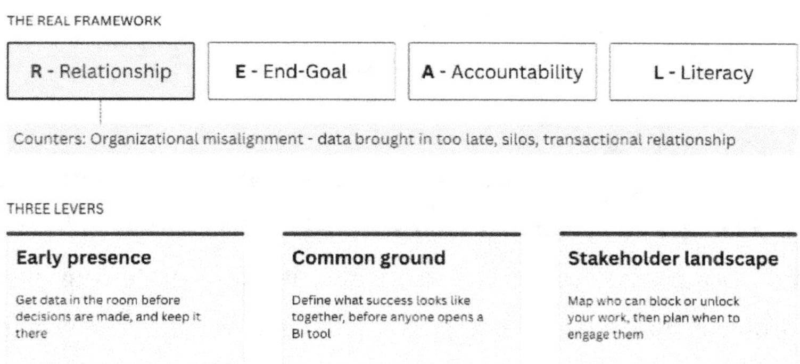

Figure 3: The three levers of the Relationship pillar, with the failure pattern each one addresses.

---

5 For more on the difference between transactional and embedded data team models, and how each affects organizational outcomes, see Thomas H. Davenport & Jeanne G. Harris, *Competing on Analytics: The New Science of Winning* (Harvard Business School Press, 2007).

Stop being the last to know

The analytics lead at the automotive company in Chapter 2 put it plainly: "They don't think to include us until execution. By then, it's too late to influence anything meaningful." She wasn't bitter about it. She'd just accepted it as the structural reality of how her team operated; summoned when something needed tracking, invisible when something was being planned. In that case, two channels underperformed badly, acquisition costs ran 40% over budget, and the campaign limped to its end with nobody willing to admit the strategy had been wrong from the start.

The data team saw all of it coming.
They just weren't in the room
when it could have mattered.

This is a story about a default set-up that nobody ever questioned, and I've seen it play out, in almost identical form, across industries and company sizes, enough times that it's stopped feeling like a problem and started feeling like a design choice nobody made consciously.

The two most common versions of dysfunction

The first one goes like this. A marketing team at a CPG company plans and launches a campaign. Creative is briefed, media is bought, and content goes live. Weeks later, someone decides it would be useful to understand how it performed, so the data team opens a ticket requesting a dashboard. The analyst opens the brief and immediately sees the problem: the tracking tags were never implemented. Nobody told the data team the campaign was happening, so nobody set up the measurement infrastructure before it launched. The data that should have been captured from day one simply doesn't exist. The dashboard gets built on whatever is available and everyone quietly agrees to call it "indicative." When budget planning comes around, the question of whether this campaign justified its spend cannot be answered properly. Numbers get cited with caveats. Decisions get made on incomplete information dressed up as analysis. The data team develops a reputation for unreliable work, even though they had no part in creating the problem.

The second example is subtler but just as damaging. A data team at a fashion scale-up receives an email in the afternoon stating that a senior leader will present to the board the following morning and needs three specific metrics included in the deck. The data team pulls the numbers and sends them over. The metrics exist, they're accurate, and they arrive in time. But nobody explained what the numbers would be used for. Nobody shared the context of the board conversation or what argument the presentation was trying to make. On the other end, the person building the deck has no idea what the numbers mean, what assumptions underlie them, what they should be compared against, or what the right interpretation is. So, they use them anyway, because they arrived on time and looked authoritative. At the board meeting, a follow-up question arises that no one can answer. Or worse, the number gets used in a way that's technically correct but contextually wrong, and nobody in the room knows enough to catch it.

In both cases, the data team did exactly what was asked and, in both cases, the outcome was worse than if data had been involved from the start. This is what exclusion costs: credibility on both sides, not just missing dashboards and incomplete metrics. The business loses trust in data because it keeps arriving too late or without enough context to be useful. The data team loses trust in the business because they keep being handed problems they can't solve properly, for reasons that have nothing to do with their capabilities.

Making early involvement easier to say yes to

Knowing that you should be included earlier doesn't tell you how to make it happen. The obstacle is a set of habits held by different people for different reasons. The argument that works with one will not work with another.

The first audience is the project owner, who sees early data involvement as friction. They're not hostile to data, but they've learned, often correctly, that involving data early means more questions, more complexity, and more meetings before anything gets done. The argument that lands isn't about data culture or best practice. It's about a specific, recognizable cost they've already paid. The CPG tracking tag story is exactly right for this conversation. The question to ask is not "Can we be involved earlier?" but "Do you remember the last time you couldn't answer a question about a campaign because the data wasn't there? That's what we're trying to prevent. We need about ten minutes at the start of the next one." That is an easier yes than asking for a structural change.

The second audience is the **senior leader** who commissions the board decks at the last minute. They don't think of data as a planning partner because they've never experienced it that way. The opportunity is usually already there in the next last-minute request. Deliver the number, then add one sentence of context: what it means for the decision at hand, what would look different if things were going well, or why the number they asked for only tells half the story. Most senior leaders have sat through at least one meeting where a number landed wrong: cited confidently, challenged immediately, and nobody could explain it. When the data team prevents that moment, people notice. That tends to be more persuasive than any amount of asking for a seat at the table.

The third audience is the **data team's own leadership**, and this is often the one that gets skipped. Getting included earlier isn't something individual analysts can negotiate for from the bottom of a ticket queue. It requires someone with enough organizational authority to propose a structural change: data on the standing agenda of sprint reviews, campaign kickoffs, and planning sessions; not as a standing presentation slot, but as a presence. The ask can be framed simply: "We want to be in the room when the questions are being set, not just when the answers are due. Can we try that for one quarter?"

Data in the room when work starts, not when it ends

Once the conversation has happened, the implementation is straightforward. The data team needs to be informed at the start of any campaign, product launch, or initiative, not when the dashboard is needed, but when the first decisions are being made. That's the moment to establish what needs to be tracked, what infrastructure needs to be in place, and what questions the data will eventually need to answer. A five-minute conversation at the beginning prevents a five-week problem at the end.

It also means that when data is requested for a high-stakes moment (a board meeting, a strategy review, a budget conversation), the request comes with context. "What is this number being used to argue?" "Who is the audience?" "What follow-up questions are likely?" The data team isn't a number-retrieval service. They're the people most qualified to make sure the number lands correctly, but only if they know what it's landing into. None of this requires a reorganization. It requires a shared understanding that data's involvement begins at the start of a process, not when someone needs an output from it.

What changes?

When early presence takes hold, the campaign tracking is in place before anything goes live, because the data team knew about the campaign and understood the requirements before it launched. The board presentation uses numbers that the data team helped frame, so the context is right, and the follow-up questions can be answered. The data team's first question when a new initiative starts isn't "When do you need the dashboard?" but "What are we trying to learn, and what do we need to set up now to be able to answer that later?" And the business team's first reflex when planning something new is to loop in data at the start, not because they were told to, but because they've seen what happens when they don't.

That shift, from data as an output to data as an input, is the whole point of early presence. And it doesn't happen because of a policy, but because the relationship is strong enough that both sides have stopped thinking of each other as separate teams doing separate jobs. But being in the room only matters if the conversation leads somewhere. That's what common ground is for.

Define success together

Being in the room early is not enough. You also need a shared definition of what you're trying to achieve, and that conversation has to happen before anyone touches the data. That retail company from Chapter 1 (the one with four dashboards all called "conversion") never had a data problem. One dashboard defined it as completed purchases, another as add-to-cart rate, a third as checkout starts, and a fourth as sessions in which users added at least one item to the cart. Nothing was technically wrong; the data was accurate, and the dashboards were polished. But product, marketing, and regional managers each had their preferred version, and they spent quarter after quarter in meetings arguing about whose numbers were right, while complaints climbed 18% and NPS fell 7 points in a single quarter. The delivery problems driving those numbers went unresolved because the conversation never got that far.

What was missing wasn't better data. It was a conversation that needed to happen before any of it was built: a shared definition of what they were trying to achieve and what they were trying to measure. That conversation can't happen productively in a review meeting, with three teams who have already staked their credibility on their version of the number.

That's what the absence of common ground looks like in practice. There was plenty of data, plenty of effort, but no shared agreement on what success meant before anyone built anything. When that conversation doesn't happen upfront, it happens later, in the worst possible setting: a review meeting, under pressure, with the actual decision waiting in the room.

The fix is not another dashboard. It is the conversation before the dashboard.

Align on the fundamentals first

A cross-functional clarity workshop is a facilitated session where all relevant teams come together (ideally before any analysis begins) to align on the fundamentals and answer basic questions as a group:

- *What are we trying to achieve?* This sounds obvious, but it rarely is. Teams that have been working together for months often discover that they've been operating with subtly different goals. Getting this answered explicitly, out loud, in the same room, is already more than most teams have done.

- *What does success look like, and how will we know when we've achieved it?* Not in abstract terms, but in observable ones. What would you see in the world if this worked? What changes, and by how much? And critically, what number would make you act? Without a defined threshold, a metric can move for weeks without generating a decision. This is the question that turns a dashboard into a compass.

- *Can we quantify the success?* Is this measurable at all? What would the metric be? This is where ambition meets reality, because teams often discover that what they care most about is also the hardest to measure. That's not a reason to abandon the goal, but it is a reason to be honest about what you're tracking.

- *Do we have the data, and can we trust it?* Where does it come from, how reliable is it, and how often does it update? A metric that sounds right but sits on top of unreliable data, or data that arrives two weeks after the decision point, isn't useful. Better to know that now than after the dashboard is built.

- *Are we all pulling in the same direction?* This is the question that closes the workshop. Each team puts its metrics on the table, not to compete, but to make visible what everyone is tracking. Together, the group sorts

> them into two tiers: overarching goals of the whole initiative, and subgoals that individual teams own in service of those. The sorting itself is often where the most important conversation happens, because teams discover that what one function treats as the primary goal, another treats as a supporting one. Getting that visible and agreed to in the room before anyone builds anything is exactly what prevents the retail conversion story from happening to you.

The output of the workshop is a **goal tree**: the overarching goals at the top, the subgoals each team owns beneath them, and the specific metrics at the bottom. One page known to all teams, built together. This becomes the single reference point for every review, every retrospective, and every conversation about whether the work is going in the right direction.

It's worth saying plainly that the workshop isn't really about metrics. It's about alignment and trust; what teams are trying to achieve together, and whether they mean the same thing when they talk about it. The questions are just a structure for a conversation that most teams never have. After that conversation, you have a team that has aligned on what success means, and that changes how data gets used far more than any dashboard ever will.

The full facilitation guide, including all five questions, is in the Field Guide under the Clarity Workshop.

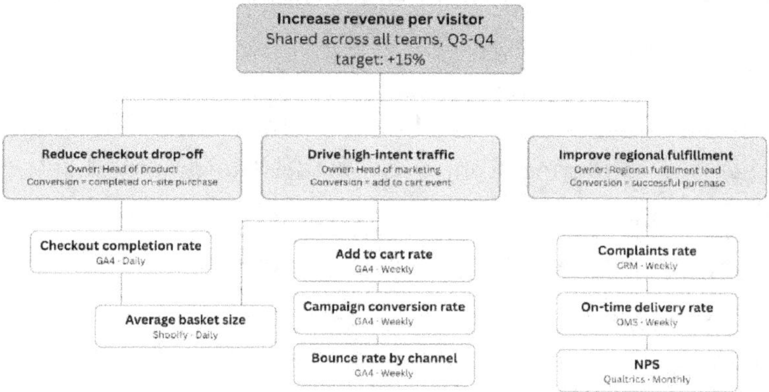

Figure 4: Goal tree output from the clarity workshop - fashion retailer. One overarching goal, three team-owned subgoals, each with its own definition of conversion and named owner. Built together, before anyone opened a BI tool.

What changes

When common ground is established, you feel it before you see it in any metric. Meetings get shorter because nobody's arguing about whose numbers are right, and decisions get made faster because everyone already agrees on what they're optimizing for. Teams come to reviews with questions about what to do next, not challenges to the data itself, and there's a quiet confidence in the room that didn't exist before, not because everything is going well, but because everyone agrees on what "going well" means. That frees the conversation up to focus on what matters: the decision in front of you.

From blockers to allies

I was brought in as a consultant to support a global automotive client in recovering from a car model launch that didn't go according to plan and to ensure the next phase went differently. The campaign was big: multiple markets, significant budget, months of preparation, and many different teams involved. Marketing held the campaign budget, sales held the targets, and regional directors held the local execution. Their centralized data team was supporting all of them, fielding requests from multiple directions, and trying to be useful to everyone at once, which, in practice, meant they were accountable to no clear owner and aligned with no single set of priorities.

The problems this created weren't visible until they became critical. In the weeks just before launch, key questions started surfacing about tracking setup, attribution, and how campaign performance would be measured across markets. Questions that nobody thought to answer earlier because nobody was responsible for asking them and because the data team wasn't in the planning conversations. By the time they were involved, it was too late to implement properly. So, the campaign went live without the necessary tracking infrastructure. Data that should have been captured from day one wasn't, and in the aftermath, when everyone wanted to understand what had worked and what hadn't, the answers weren't there. The loss wasn't just analytical; it was also relational. The marketing team lost confidence in the data function, and the data team felt set up to fail. Both were right, in their way.

The fix wasn't technical. There were no data quality problems or capability gaps. It was a planning problem. The project team had never mapped who makes decisions on this initiative, and when they need to be involved for it to matter. Once we had that, we built the data team's involvement backward from those moments. Tracking infrastructure was agreed upon during requirements. Check-ins with the marketing budget holders happened at four defined points during preparation: not to present findings, but to confirm alignment and surface anything that had shifted. By launch day, no critical questions were outstanding.

The difference wasn't the quality of the analysis. It was knowing who needed to be involved, and when.

Map the landscape, then plan when to connect

Not everyone needs the same level of involvement. Some stakeholders need the details because their decisions depend on understanding the data. Others just need updates, because they want to know things are on track without being pulled into every conversation. Treating everyone the same wastes everyone's time and, more importantly, means the people who need deep engagement don't get it.

The practical starting point is an influence map, built by the project team together at the start of any major initiative. The two questions are simple: "Who has influence over this initiative?" and

"Who has an interest in its outcomes?" Plotting both dimensions together tells you something more useful than an org chart ever could; not who is senior, but who can block progress and who can unlock it.

Figure 5: Influence map for the Stakeholder landscape lever. Plotting influence against interest reveals not who is most senior, but who can block progress and who can unlock it. The goal is not just to map where stakeholders are - it is to move them. High-influence, low-interest stakeholders are not a permanent fixture; shifting them to the right is where the real leverage lies.

The four quadrants each call for a different kind of engagement:

- **Key players** (high influence, high interest) are your most important relationships. These are the budget holders and decision makers who are already engaged. Keep them close, involve them early, and make sure they're never surprised.

- **Build interest** (high influence, low interest) is where the most important and most neglected work happens.

These are the people with the power to act on your work, or quietly ignore it, who don't yet see why they should care. Getting them engaged is harder than maintaining an existing relationship, but it's where the real leverage lies.

- **Keep engaged** (low influence, high interest) are your enthusiastic allies. They can't move the needle on their own, but they amplify the work and often influence the people who can.

- **Minimal effort** (low influence, low interest) monitor, but don't over-invest.

One thing the map doesn't show, but the text needs to say: the goal isn't just to plot where people are, it's to move them. The high-influence, low-interest stakeholders sitting in "build interest" are not a permanent fixture; they're a challenge. Part of the data team's job is to shift them rightward over time by making the value of engagement visible and relevant to the things they care about.

Once you know who matters, the other half is timing. An engagement timeline is a simple plan of who needs to be in the room at which moments, built in advance so the right conversations happen before decisions get made. Most blockers that derail work at the finish line are entirely predictable. They just aren't planned for.

The situation in Figure 6 is just one very simple example. Every initiative is different; some will need more touchpoints, some fewer, some will involve different people at different stages. The specific meetings matter less than the principle behind them: plan the engagement in advance, match the right people to the right moments, and make sure nobody is hearing critical information for the first time at the end.

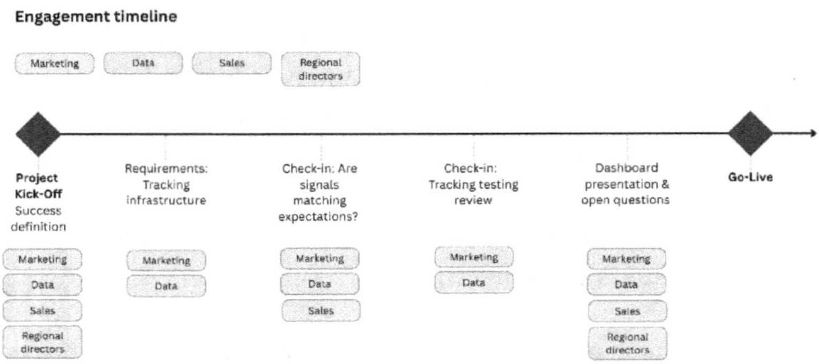

Figure 6: Engagement timeline from the automotive campaign. Tracking infrastructure agreed at the requirements stage, two structured check-ins during preparation, and a final dashboard presentation to close all open questions before go-live. Marketing and the data team present throughout; sales and regional directors are brought in when their input is needed.

These are two simple tools, but they change something fundamental. When the right message reaches the right person at the right time, stakeholders stop being blockers and become allies. They defend the data in meetings you're not in. They pull you into conversations before you even know they are happening.

What changes

At the start of any major initiative, the project team has a clear picture of who needs what and when. Tracking is tested and in place before anything goes live, and engagement is planned, not improvised. When results come in, nobody's surprised or skeptical, because they've been part of the story all along. That's the difference between data that influences decisions and data that gets filed away.

Conclusion

The ticket-in, report-out dynamic persists in most organizations, not because people want it to, but because nobody has deliberately designed an alternative. Data teams fill the role they're given, business teams work with the model they've always used, and the status quo reproduces itself one unopened dashboard at a time.

A relationship breaks this cycle by changing the structural position of data within how work gets done. **Early presence** means data is in the room when decisions are still open. **Common ground** means teams have defined goals and success criteria. **Stakeholder landscape** makes sure the right people are never surprised. The shift they produce isn't just operational, but relational. When a data team is embedded early in planning, they stop being the people who build things and start being the people who help decide things. That changes how their work is treated, how their recommendations land, and how much the organization is willing to invest in the function over time.

There's a version of this I watched unfold at a telecommunications company where I worked sporadically over three years. When I started, the data team ran a ticket queue: requests came in from five different business units, outputs went out, and nobody was particularly satisfied. By the time I stopped working with them, two of those business units had embedded data leads attending their weekly planning sessions. Those leads were co-authoring the briefs that went to leadership, not building reports to attach to them. The data hadn't changed, nor had the team's technical capability. What changed was the moment in the process when data appeared, and with it, the kinds of questions data could help answer.

The first planning session one of those leads attended wasn't particularly dramatic. She told me later she didn't say much. She listened to what the business lead was scoping, and then asked, at the end: "What would make you change course on this mid-campaign?" The business lead paused. It was quite a basic question, but nobody had asked it before. The person who should have been asking it had always been handed the brief after the decisions were already made.

What I've noticed, after watching this play out across a number of organizations, is that when data teams are included early, the business teams often relax. Not because the data is better, but because they're no longer alone with the problem. That matters more than most people expect. But a different conversation only gets you so far if nobody's clear on what the conversation is trying to decide. That's the gap Relationship can't close on its own, and it's what End-goal is for.

CHAPTER 5

End-goal

The most dangerous dashboard request is the one that sounds reasonable.

"Can you track campaign performance?"
"Yes, of course."
"Can you build a view of our key metrics?"
"Absolutely."

The request is clear, the ask is specific, and the deadline is manageable. And yet, three weeks later, the dashboard exists, and nobody knows what to do with it, because the one question nobody asked was:

"What are we supposed to decide with this?"

I've sat in many review meetings where people look at a screen full of numbers, nodding, yet nobody says what they're going to do differently. Not because the data is wrong, but because the dashboard was built to show what's happening, not to answer the question that matters: "Given what we're seeing, what do we do next?"[6] That is strategic ambiguity in its most common form. Not dramatic confusion about direction, but the quiet kind, where goals exist on paper and never make it into what the data team actually builds.

That gap between the data that exists and the decisions that get made is what End-goal is about. It's the second failure pattern from Part I: strategic ambiguity. Not dramatic ambiguity, the quiet kind, where the goals exist on paper but never make it into what the data team builds. The dashboard tracks sessions, conversions, and revenue, but the decision it needs to support is whether to reallocate budget from acquisition to retention. Those are not the same question, and a dashboard designed for one cannot answer the other.

This is where End-goal diverges from common ground. Common ground is about getting teams to agree on what success looks like before anyone builds anything - the shared definition, the goal tree, the conversation that should have happened before the first dashboard request arrived. End-goal operates one step later, in the moment of commission: when someone asks for a report, a

---

[6] For more on why information alone rarely drives action, and what makes the difference between ideas that stick and ideas that don't, see Chip Heath & Dan Heath, *Made to Stick: Why Some Ideas Survive and Others Die* (Random House, 2007).

dashboard, or an analysis, and the first question should be "What decision is this going to support?" but seldom is.

Common ground sets the destination.

End-goal makes sure the vehicle is pointed at it.

The fix has three levers. **Decision-first** is about asking the decision question before any analysis starts, so that what gets built is designed around an outcome rather than an output. **Designed for people** is about building data products for what real people need to do, not just what they want to see, because a dashboard built for a CFO and a dashboard built for a campaign manager are not the same thing, even if they're tracking the same numbers. And finally, **Packaged for action** is about delivering insights in a form that moves people from information to action, not from meeting to meeting.

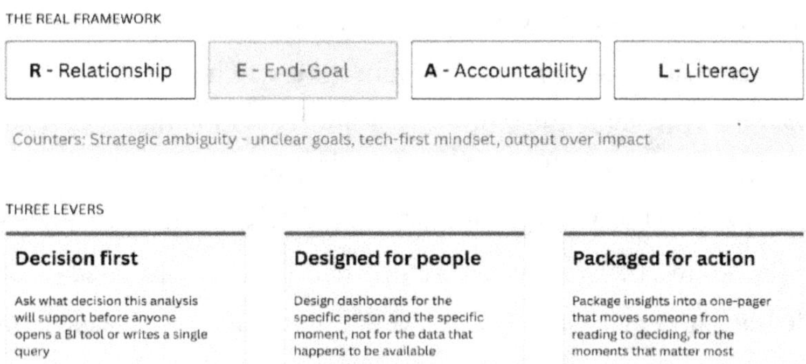

Figure 7: The three levers of the End-goal pillar, with the failure pattern each one addresses.

What makes this hard is the discipline of stopping when someone asks for a dashboard and says, "Before we build anything, what are you going to decide with it?" That question feels disruptive because it slows things down at the start, but it's the only thing that reliably prevents building something nobody uses.

Start with the decision. Everything else follows from that.

Start with the why, not the data

A telecoms client asked me to build a churn model. A classic request, entirely predictable for that industry at the time. Every major telco has one; most are technically sophisticated, and churn is as close to an existential problem as that business gets. The brief arrived well-formatted, the deadline was reasonable, and it felt like exactly the sort of thing a data team should be working on. It also felt familiar. The previous year's churn model had produced a ranked list of 40,000 at-risk subscribers. The retention team worked through the top few hundred, ran their standard reactivation outreach, and saw no measurable impact. Nobody had asked why. The model was technically solid, the process had been followed, and the low return had been quietly filed under "Churn is hard." So, before we started building, I asked one question: "If we predict who's going to churn, what will you actually do?"

Silence. Then, thinking out loud. The question hadn't been asked before, but once it was on the table, people had things to say about it. The conversation that followed was the kind that rarely happens in project kickoffs: honest, a little uncomfortable, and genuinely useful. They couldn't intervene for everyone because the subscriber base was too large, and the retention team was too stretched. A raw list of at-risk customers wouldn't help much if there was no way to prioritize who deserved attention or which outreach made sense for each segment. Prediction alone wasn't actionable. So, we kept talking, pulled out a whiteboard, and spent the next hour working backward from what they could do rather than what they thought they needed to measure.

The reframe that came out of that conversation was simple: not "Who will churn?" but "Who is at risk, and still savable?" That shift changed everything about what we built. The output wasn't a model; it was a prioritization tool for the retention team that identified the customers most likely to leave and most likely to respond to intervention, and ranked them accordingly. Six months later, retention was 7% higher than in the previous comparable period, worth roughly €4M in revenue. Not because the data science was more sophisticated, but because the question behind it was more honest.

Four questions that eliminate half your dashboard requests

Most analytics work starts in the wrong place. Someone needs a dashboard, a report, or a model, and the first question that gets asked is "What data do we have?" or "How should we build this?"

The question that should come first, and rarely does, is simpler and considerably more inconvenient: "What decision are we trying to make?"

When analysis starts from the data rather than the decision, you get dashboards that answer questions nobody asked, and presentations where the analyst walks through fifteen slides of findings. The room nods politely, but nobody knows what to do next.

The churn model story is not unusual. I see versions of it constantly. Teams request analysis based on what sounds useful rather than what they've committed to doing. Analysts build based on what's technically feasible rather than what's needed, and the gap between those two starting points is where most data work quietly dies.

The tool I use to close that gap is called the decision backward brief, and it's deliberately simple. Before any analysis begins, before requirements are gathered, before anyone opens a BI tool, the analyst and the stakeholder answer four questions together:

- *What decision needs to be made, and by when?* This question forces specificity. "Improve our marketing performance" is not a decision. "Decide by the end of Q2 whether to shift 30% of our paid social budget to email nurture, based on cost-per-acquisition trends" is. The harder version of this question is the one worth sitting with: "If the data tells us something we didn't want to hear, what changes?"

- *Who is making that decision?* Not the team, but a named individual, who will be held to it. (We'll go deeper on why this matters in Chapter 6: Accountability.)

- *What do we already know?* This prevents teams from spending three weeks producing analysis that confirms what everyone already believes, and surfaces the assumptions that need testing.

- *What format will help us act on it?* Deciding on the output format up front clarifies who needs to do what with the results. A ranked list is different from a trend line, and a recommendation is different from a summary of findings.

The brief takes about 30 minutes the first time, and 10 minutes once people are used to it. It's not a formal document requiring sign-off. It's a conversation with a short written record. Some of my clients have built it directly into their ticketing system, so every analytics request starts with a version of these questions; others use it as a planning conversation before building. Either way: simple questions, significant clarity.

Detailed guidelines are in the Field Guide under the Decision Backward Brief.

The Decision backward brief

Answer these four questions before any analysis begins

What decision needs to be made, and by when?

Which at-risk subscribers should the retention team contact, and what kind of outreach makes sense for each segment, prioritized for the next retention cycle.

Who is making that decision?

The head of the retention team, who owns the outreach budget and capacity.

What do we already know?

We know the churn already. What we don't know is who is still savable, and the retention team is too stretched to intervene for everyone.

What format will help us act on it?

A prioritization tool: a ranked list of at-risk customers most likely to respond to intervention, with segment context that the team can act on directly.

Figure 8: The decision backward brief captures the four questions that must be answered before any analysis begins. The worked example shows a retention team prioritizing at-risk subscribers for outreach.

Two objections come up reliably. The first is honest: "We don't always know what decision we're making yet. Sometimes we need to explore first." This is true and worth taking seriously. Exploratory analysis is real and valuable. The brief accommodates this. In an exploratory context, the question shifts slightly: not "What is the decision?" but "What decision might this exploration eventually enable?" Even then, there's usually a set of choices the findings could inform, and starting there still beats starting from "what does our data warehouse contain?"

The second objection is political: asking a senior stakeholder "What decision are you making?" can feel like a challenge rather than a question. The framing that tends to work better is: "Help me understand what you'd do differently depending on what we find." Most people prefer clarity to confrontation. And the ones who find it genuinely threatening are usually the ones whose decision is already made and who want analysis for decoration rather than direction, which is useful to know as early as possible.

When decision-first is working, the nature of analytics requests changes. Instead of "Can you build a dashboard tracking campaign performance?" the request over time becomes "We need to decide by the end of the month whether to continue investing in this channel; what would we need to see to make that call confidently?" Analysts spend less time going back for clarification and more time building what matters. Stakeholders start thinking about some of the issues before they arrive because they know the question is coming. And the work that gets done is more likely to connect to a real decision, because it was designed around one from the start. The churn model story ends with €4M in recovered revenue, but the more important outcome was quieter: a data team that was finally being asked the right question, and a business team that finally knew how to ask it.

Decision-first gets the questions right. The next lever makes sure the answers reach the right person in the right form.

Dashboards for real people

I was brought in to help a media company understand why its newly built analytics platform wasn't getting used. They had built it properly: solid infrastructure, a clean interface, well-organized metrics, and role-based access. By every technical measure, it was a good product; however, adoption was around 15% after six months, and the data team was quietly frustrated and openly confused.

I spent a morning running stakeholder interviews with four different people who had access to the platform: a campaign manager, a regional sales director, a content editor, and a CFO. It was not a requirements session; more like a pain-point conversation to help me understand their situation. I asked each of them about their decision-making process, where they got stuck, what they wished they had, and what they ended up asking a colleague because they couldn't find it themselves. And then, the question that tends to cut through everything: "When you open this dashboard, what are you actually trying to figure out?" This kind of structured listening session is something any data team can run with any mix of stakeholders.

The campaign manager wanted to know whether to pause a specific ad set before the weekend, the sales director wanted to walk into his next meeting knowing which accounts needed immediate attention, the content editor wanted to understand which stories were worth commissioning more of, and the CFO wanted a single number she could defend to the board without a 30-minute explanation.

None of them needed the same thing, yet the platform had been built as if they did. A comprehensive view of everything, organized by data category, designed for completeness rather than for any of the four actual people sitting in front of me. It was relevant to the data, but not to the people.

Build from the person first, not the data

Decision-first refines the question, and Designed for people shapes the answer - a dashboard or data product that connects directly to what a specific person needs to do, not just what they might find interesting to see. The distinction sounds small, but the consequences are not.

Most dashboards are built from the data outward: here is what we have, here is how it's structured, here is a reasonably logical way to display it. The implicit assumption is that users will find their way to what matters. Some will, but most won't.[7] Not because they're incapable, but because they're busy and looking at a screen that wasn't designed with their specific job in mind. The CMO, the product manager, and the CFO all make different decisions, and yet most dashboards treat them the same way.

---

[7] For more on why designing for the system's logic rather than the user's mental model consistently produces tools people don't use, see Don Norman, *The Design of Everyday Things* (Basic Books, 1988; revised edition 2013).

Building for the person first (their role, decisions, daily reality) and working backward from the data flips that logic entirely. It starts with a person, a role, and a moment: "What is this person trying to decide or do, what would make that easier, and what is the fastest path from opening this dashboard to taking that action?"[8] Everything else (every metric, every filter, every visualization) is either in service of that or it isn't.

The structured way to get there is what I call the Dashboard Design Workshop. It's a design thinking-inspired session, run with or without stakeholders, before any dashboard is built. It's not a requirements gathering meeting, but rather a structured exploration of what each person needs to act. The questions are organized around four themes:

- **Context and environment**: Where and when does this person use data, and what does that moment look like in practice?
- **Current behavior**: What do they do today when they don't have the information they need, and when was the last time data genuinely changed what they did?
- **Goals and needs**: What are they trying to achieve, what slows them down, and what would they be able to do differently if the dashboard worked perfectly?

---

[8] For more on designing data products around what users need to do rather than what data is available to show, see Stephen Few, *Now You See It: Simple Visualization Techniques for Quantitative Analysis* (Analytics Press, 2009).

- **Fear and trust**: What would make them ignore it entirely, and what would make them trust a number enough to stake a decision on it?

That last theme is the one most teams skip, and it's usually where the most useful answers live. Once you have responses across all four, dashboards almost build themselves, because everyone gets what they need, not noise. And that's when dashboards start driving decisions. The full facilitation guide and question bank are in the Field Guide under the Dashboard Design Workshop.

Three weeks after the redesign went live, I got a message from the data lead. The CFO, who had previously needed a 30-minute briefing before she could use any number in a board presentation, had sent the team a one-line note: "I'm taking this to the board. The methodology is clear." No meeting request, no "Can someone talk me through this?" Just that. That was when I knew it had worked.

Weekly active use at the media company went from 15% to over 60% in two quarters. The data and the platform didn't change; what changed was that the dashboards finally reflected the work the people using them were trying to do. When dashboards are designed for people, you stop hearing "I have the dashboard, but I still don't know what to do." People open it because it answers a question they have. The campaign manager pauses the ad set before the weekend without waiting for a weekly report. The sales director walks into a meeting knowing exactly which three accounts need immediate attention. The CFO stops asking for explanations and starts asking for implications. Requests to the data team become more specific because stakeholders now know what they need and that the team can deliver it. That's not a small thing. It's the difference between a data team that gets pulled into decisions and one that gets pulled in after them.

Turn analysis into a decision

I supported a retailer through their Christmas campaign. These three to four weeks are their busiest and most important period of the year. There was limited time, a significant budget, and decisions that needed to be made quickly. There was no room for lengthy review cycles or weekly reports that arrived two days after the moment had passed. Every week counted, and every budget reallocation needed to happen before the opportunity closed.

Before we introduced the brief, their reviews looked like this: the marketing manager would open the dashboard, scroll through ROAS by channel, and say something like "I think Display is underperforming, but I'm not sure if that's a creative issue or a placement one." Someone would pull up a different tab. Someone else would offer to dig into it. By the time anyone had an answer, it was another day. The decision window, the one where reallocating budget to the right channel would have actually mattered, had already closed.

Knowing their goals and KPIs in advance, we prepared a one-page weekly Budget Optimization Brief. One page that showed what had happened, what had changed, and what to do next. The marketing manager could open it and immediately decide "Reallocate €40K from Display to Meta." Done. No meeting to schedule, no dashboard to interpret, no analyst to chase for context. The brief had already done that work.

That one-pager cut review meetings by more than half and improved ROAS by roughly 15% over the course of the campaign. By the end of the campaign, that translated to over €1M in extra sales, not because the data was better than the year before, but because everyone knew exactly what mattered and exactly what to do with it.

Five components that turn analysis into a decision

Packaged for action is more selective than the previous two levers. Use it in the moments that matter most: a high-stakes campaign, a critical product launch, a budget review where timing is everything. Not every project needs an action brief. A routine weekly report and an exploratory analysis don't. But when the stakes are high enough that getting the format wrong has a real cost, this is the tool.

The format itself is called the action brief, and it has five components:[9]

- **Situation**: What is happening and why it matters right now. Not background, not history, just the single most important thing the reader needs to understand before anything else. One sentence, if possible.

- **Status**: Are we on track or not? This is the factual layer: KPIs against targets, actual versus planned, a RAG view if that's how the team works. No interpretation yet, just a clear picture of where things stand.

- **Insights:** The two or three findings most relevant to the decision; what the numbers are telling us and not just what they show. The selection should reflect what the decision hinges on, not just what supports a preferred direction.

- **Action:** What to do now. When the data points clearly in one direction and the team has enough context to back it up, own it - not "The data suggests we might consider" but a direct position. When the picture is genuinely mixed, or when the data team is working with incomplete context, present two or three options with a clear steer on which looks stronger and why, and be explicit about what's missing. The goal either way is to

---

[9] The structure adapts Barbara Minto's Situation-Complication-Question-Answer framework, which remains the most rigorous approach to structuring communication for decision-makers. See Barbara Minto, *The Pyramid Principle: Logic in Writing and Thinking* (Pearson, 1987; updated 2008).

move the reader toward a decision, not to hand the question back unanswered.

- **Risk:** What could go wrong, or what the data doesn't yet tell us. This is not a disclaimer; it's a signal that the person who wrote this thought carefully enough about the recommendation to anticipate the challenge to it.

One thing worth saying explicitly: producing a brief like this is only possible if the data team has been in the room from the start. Not brought in when the campaign is already live and asked to report on what's happening, but present when the goals were set, the plan was made, and the KPIs were agreed.

During the Christmas campaign, we could produce a useful one-pager every week precisely because we knew the full context: what the targets were, what had been tried, what the budget constraints looked like, and what decisions the marketing manager had the authority to make. Without that context, the brief becomes guesswork dressed up as a recommendation. This is why Relationship, the first pillar of REAL, is a precondition for Packaged for action rather than a nice-to-have alongside it. You can't package insights for action if you were never close enough to the work to understand what action is even possible.

A blank template and guidance notes are in the Field Guide under the Action Brief.

A brief written to this structure takes a good analyst about an hour to produce once the underlying analysis is done. It takes a decision-maker about five minutes to read, and unlike a deck full of findings with no conclusion, it answers the question before anyone has to ask it.

X-Mas Campaign Week 3
Budget reallocation

Budget remaining
€180K
of €880K total

Overall ROAS
3.2x
Target 3.5x

Revenue generated
€2.24M
Target €3.08M

CHANNEL STATUS · TARGET ROAS 3.5x

CHANNEL	SPEND €	ROAS	vs TARGET	STATUS NOTE	ACTION
Email	42K	6.2x	77%	Highest ROAS. List nearly exhausted for the season.	Hold
Meta	185K	4.6x	31%	Above target. Inventory available. Tested at 4.1x this quarter.	+40K €
Paid Search	245K	4.1x	17%	Stable. CPC rising slightly in final week — watch closely.	Hold
Affiliate	98K	3.1x	-11%	Voucher activity compressing margin. Monitor.	Monitor
Display	130K	1.8x	-49%	Underperformed all 3 weeks. No recovery trend.	Pause

On or above target · Within 15% of target · More than 15% below target

INSIGHT
The campaign is ahead of the blended ROAS target. We should protect and extend the lead in the final week. Display is consuming €130K of budget at 1.8x while Meta is delivering 4.6x with inventory still available.

RECOMMENDED ACTION
Reallocate **€40K from Display to Meta** immediately. Pause remaining Display spend. Review remaining €140K allocation by Wednesday

RISK TO WATCH
Meta inventory may tighten in the final week given competitor activity. If CPM rises above €18, reassess reallocation volume.

Figure 9: A worked action brief example for a Christmas campaign. Numbers are illustrative. The actual campaign cut review meetings by more than half and delivered over €1M in additional sales.

The most common objection is also the most legitimate: "What if I'm wrong?" Making a recommendation means being accountable for it, and that feels risky, especially when the person on the other side of the table is more senior. But a vague analysis that gets ignored has no impact at all. A clear recommendation that gets challenged, debated, or even rejected has moved the conversation forward.

Being wrong in a productive way is more useful than being safe in a way that changes nothing.

Decision-makers don't expect analysts to be infallible; they expect them to be honest about their reasoning, which the brief's risk section is specifically designed to show.

The second objection is practical: some analyses genuinely don't support a single recommendation because the data is inconclusive, or the trade-offs are genuinely complex. The brief accommodates this, too. The recommendation section can say: "The data doesn't yet support a clear direction; here is what we'd need to resolve that, and by when." That is still a recommendation. It recommends a next step rather than a final decision, and it's infinitely more useful than a deck that ends with "Further analysis may be required."

When Packaged for Action is in place, the analysis shapes what happens next.

When insights are packaged for action, data stops being something people check after the fact and becomes something that accelerates decisions when it really matters. Meetings get shorter because the first 20 minutes aren't spent establishing a shared understanding of the findings. The marketing manager doesn't wait for a weekly report; she acts on a one-pager that already tells her what to do. Decision-makers start treating the data team as advisors rather than reporters, because the team has stopped reporting and started advising. And the analysis that took weeks to produce doesn't disappear into a folder; it shapes what happens next, which is what it was built to do in the first place.

There's a broader shift underneath this worth naming plainly. Most data teams are trained to be neutral, to present the evidence and protect their credibility by not overreaching. That neutrality has its place, but in high-stakes moments, the most valuable thing a data team can do is have an honest and reasoned point of view. Not a reckless or overconfident one, but a clearly evidenced position on what the data means for the decision in front of the room.

Conclusion

Strategic ambiguity persists in most organizations not because people are comfortable with vagueness, but because no one has given them a practical way out. Asking a clear decision question before analysis starts feels disruptive, designing dashboards for specific people and specific moments feels like extra work, and packaging findings into a direct recommendation feels risky. So, teams skip all three, build for completeness instead of clarity, and then wonder why the data never quite shapes the decisions it was supposed to support.

End-goal breaks that cycle by changing what gets built and why. Decision-first means every piece of analysis starts with a decision rather than a dataset, so the work has a destination before it begins. Designed for people means dashboards are built for what real people need to make decisions, not what seems comprehensive from the data team's perspective. Packaged for action means the right insights reach the right person at the right moment, in a format that moves them from understanding to deciding.

All three levers assume one thing that the end goal itself can't guarantee: that when the decision gets made, someone feels responsible for what happens next. You can build the most precise, decision-ready analysis in the room and still watch it dissolve into vague agreement and deferred action, because the meeting ended without anyone's name attached to the outcome. Getting clear on the decision is necessary, but owning it is what makes it stick. That's what Accountability is for.

Chapter 6

Accountability

A metric has been slowly declining for weeks, and different teams have seen it because it's on the dashboard and has come up in several meetings. Yet when I ask who is responsible for fixing it, the room goes quiet in a very particular way. Not because nobody cares, but because everyone assumed someone else was handling it. That moment is what operational gaps look like in practice. It's an ownership failure, where responsibility for acting on what the data shows is spread so thinly across functions that it effectively belongs to nobody. Dashboards are updated, reports circulate, numbers are discussed, and when the meeting ends, nobody has a job to do.

Accountability is the third pillar of REAL and the direct countermove to operational gaps. Not the kind that appears on company values slides, but more concrete and operational, built around three levers. **Ownership** gives every key metric a single named person responsible for what happens when it moves.

Shared language makes sure everyone understands the number the same way. And **cadence** creates the recurring moment in which the owner must interpret the metric and decide what happens next. When those three conditions exist, data stops decorating the conversation and starts driving it. None of the three works without the other two. An owner without trusted numbers hedges. Trusted numbers without an owner go unactioned. Both without a recurring moment to surface them, stay theoretical.

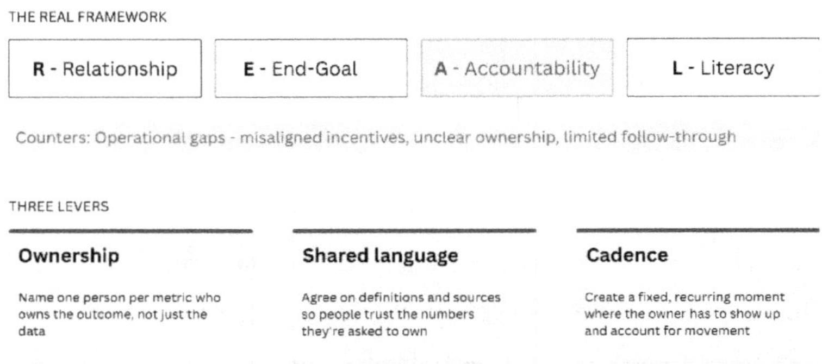

Figure 10: The three levers of the Accountability pillar, with the failure pattern each one addresses.

Give every KPI a face

I was working with a household brand from a global CPG company on their Customer Experience (CX) data when I noticed the complaints resolution rate in Western Europe had been declining for months. Not dramatically (a percentage point or two at a time), but continuously, across 40 markets, which translated into tens of thousands of unresolved complaints. Their VP of CX was genuinely proud of what they had built: complaint volume by product category, resolution times by region, escalation rates, repeat complainants, and several other metrics, all updating daily and accessible to anyone with a login. The data wasn't the problem. When the decline appeared in three different weekly reports, came up in leadership meetings, and made it onto a slide deck for the regional review, nothing happened. I asked the VP of Customer Experience who was responsible for fixing it. She said Customer Service set the response protocols. I asked Customer Service, and they said Quality needed to sign off on any resolution involving product defects. Quality said Supply Chain controlled the replacement timelines, and Supply Chain said they were operating within the parameters Marketing had approved for that product line. Marketing said this was an operational issue, not a brand one. Five functions, zero owners.

The structure makes it easy for responsibility to spread thin and disappear. When a metric crosses functional boundaries, everyone has a plausible reason why it belongs to someone else, and the more functions it touches, the more convincing each reason sounds. I brought it to the VP's attention, and we agreed to get the right people in a room to work through three questions: "Who owns this outcome?" "What does movement in this metric require in terms of action?" "Who needs to be informed and when?" The mapping took about 20 minutes. The harder conversation was what ownership meant: not producing the report, not presenting the number in meetings, but explaining why it moved and leading the response.

The first Metric Review after the owner was named was uncomfortable, as accountability meetings always are when they're new. She came in having actually looked at the numbers beforehand, which sounds obvious, but wasn't how these conversations had worked before. She had a theory about what was driving the decline in one region. It was wrong, but the fact that she had a theory, that she arrived with a position rather than a shrug, changed the entire texture of the conversation. Someone was responsible, and everyone in the room could feel it. Within one quarter of having a named owner, resolution rates were back above 65%, after months of steady decline. Nothing structural had changed. Just one person who now felt the number as theirs, and that turned out to matter more than any of the reporting infrastructure beneath it.

The output of that conversation is what I now call an Ownership Map - a simple document that names the owner of each key metric, defines what threshold triggers escalation, and specifies the review frequency. It does not need to be complicated; a spreadsheet with four columns is enough to start.

Give every metric a name and a face

Ownership means one named person per key metric who is responsible for the outcome, not the data.[10] Most companies have data owners, but far fewer have metric owners. They are not the same thing. A data owner manages the pipeline, the definition, and the refresh schedule. A metric owner is accountable for what the number represents, and they are the ones who explain why it moved, what is being done about it, and what happens next.

Where this gets stuck is predictable. The first objection is always collective: this metric spans multiple functions, so ownership must be shared. It sounds reasonable, but it doesn't work. Shared ownership is the organizational equivalent of no ownership, because it distributes responsibility so widely that nobody feels it. The goal is to name one person accountable for the conversation when it moves, not to pretend that only one team influences a metric. Influence can be shared, accountability cannot.

The second place it gets stuck is in confusing seniority with ownership. The most senior person in the room is not automatically the right owner.

---

[10] The principle of named accountability for outcomes rather than activities has a long precedent in management practice. Grove argued that every output in an organization should have a single owner responsible for results (not tasks, or reporting, but the outcome itself). When ownership is collective, it is effectively absent. For more, see Andrew S. Grove, *High Output Management* (Random House, 1983).

The right owner is the person with the most direct ability to understand the metric, diagnose movement, and mobilize a response.

Sometimes that is a VP, but often it is not.

Metric	Owner	What movement requires	Who to inform	Escalation threshold	Review frequency
Complaints resolution rate	VP Consumer Experience	Review resolution protocols with Customer Service; escalate product defects to Quality	Chief Operating Officer, Regional Directors	Drop below 65%	Biweekly
Repeat complaint rate	Head of Customer Service	Investigate root cause; brief Quality and Supply Chain	VP Consumer Experience	Rise above 12%	Monthly
Resolution time (days)	Customer Service Operations Lead	Review staffing levels and protocol bottlenecks	VP Consumer Experience	Exceeds 5 days	Weekly

Figure 11: KPI owner overview, worked example. Each row assigns a single named owner to a single metric, specifies the action required for that movement, who needs to be informed, the threshold that triggers escalation, and how frequently the metric is reviewed. Without a named person, the remaining columns have nothing to anchor to.

What changes

The clearest signal that ownership is working is behavioral and it shows up in meetings: when a metric moves, one person speaks first, not to defend their function, but to explain what they know, what they do not know yet, and what they are doing about it. That person was not assigned to present; they spoke because it's theirs.

You also see it in how questions get asked. In organizations without clear ownership, a declining metric sparks debate over which number is correct, whose methodology is right, and whether the data can really be trusted. In organizations where ownership is in place, the same declining metric generates a different conversation: "What happened, what does it mean, and what is the decision?"

The ownership map template, including the three questions and table format, is in the Field Guide under the Ownership Map.

At the CPG company, the mapping session produced an ownership map covering 14 key metrics across CX, Quality, and Supply Chain. Three of those metrics had previously had no named owner. Six had ownership assigned to a department rather than a person. Within one quarter of the map being in place, most of the tracked metrics had started moving in the right direction, not because the business had fundamentally changed, but because someone now felt responsible for explaining the ones that had not.

That shift from "The data team tracks this" to "I'm responsible for this," is the difference between a team where a metric can decline for twelve weeks while five functions explain why it belongs to someone else, and a team where one person speaks first when the number moves. Metrics stop being things the data team tracks and start being things business people are responsible for. That transition, from data as reporting to data as accountability, is what makes the rest of the framework possible. But there is a condition: ownership only works when people trust the numbers they are being asked to own. A named owner who privately isn't sure how the metric is calculated, or who knows that Finance and Marketing are working from different definitions of the same KPI, will not behave like an owner. They will hedge, qualify, and quietly pass the conversation back to the data team. Before ownership can stick, shared language has to be in place.

Build trust through clarity

A large multinational retailer I worked with had separate teams for e-commerce, in-store operations, and regional buying across multiple European markets. All of them were tracking retention; however, they never agreed on what it meant. When it appeared on the quarterly review agenda, flagged as a concern that needed a proper conversation, the e-commerce lead opened at 67%, the loyalty program manager at 71%, and Finance at 58%. What followed was 40 minutes of debate about whose methodology was correct, which data source was most reliable, and whether a 90-day purchase window was a reasonable definition or an arbitrary one. By the time the meeting ended, the question of what to do about retention had never come up.

The mechanism is the same every time. There is no shared definition established upfront, so the conversation gets stuck on the numbers rather than on what to do about them. And it's entirely preventable.

At the retailer, it was a metrics glossary: eight metrics, one agreed definition each, the formulas written out in plain language, the data source named, and the owner identified. It took three weeks to build and required two difficult conversations about whose definition would win.

The next quarterly review opened with one retention number. The methodology debate lasted a couple of minutes, and the remaining time was spent on what to do about it - specifically, reallocating budget toward lapsed customer reactivation, something that had been sitting on the table for two quarters without ever getting traction because nobody could agree on who the lapsed customers were.

The shared language that makes accountability possible

What the metrics glossary built was basic governance. This is not an enterprise data governance architecture. It is the minimum foundation that makes accountability work in real meetings: shared definitions, named sources, visible formulas, and stewards who maintain them. Most teams waiting for the full governance program to arrive before they start making better decisions are waiting too long. You can change how meetings go now, without a steering committee or a six-month project plan.

The starting point is almost always the **metrics glossary**: one agreed definition per metric, the formula written out in plain English, the data source named, the owner identified. It produces the most immediate and visible result. When a leadership team stops debating whose retention number is correct and starts discussing what to do about it, people notice, and that shift builds the appetite for everything that follows.

Open formulas make the calculation behind every key metric visible and accessible. In most companies, metrics are black boxes: the number appears in the dashboard, but the logic behind it lives in a spreadsheet owned by an analyst years ago. When it moves unexpectedly, nobody can interrogate it. Open formulas remove that dependency, and therefore remove the excuse.

A **single source of truth dashboards** is where key metrics live, from which every report and every slide draws. Not a number exported last week and reformatted, not a figure calculated slightly differently because different BI tools have different default date ranges. One source, one number, one conversation.

Named stewards are people responsible for maintaining each metric's definition, formula, and source. Not owning the outcome; that is the metric owner. Owning the definition. When something looks wrong, the steward is the first to call.

These four quick wins do not need to be implemented simultaneously. Start with the glossary and cover the eight to twelve metrics that appear most frequently in leadership conversations. Get those right, watch what changes in the room, and let that momentum pull the next step forward.

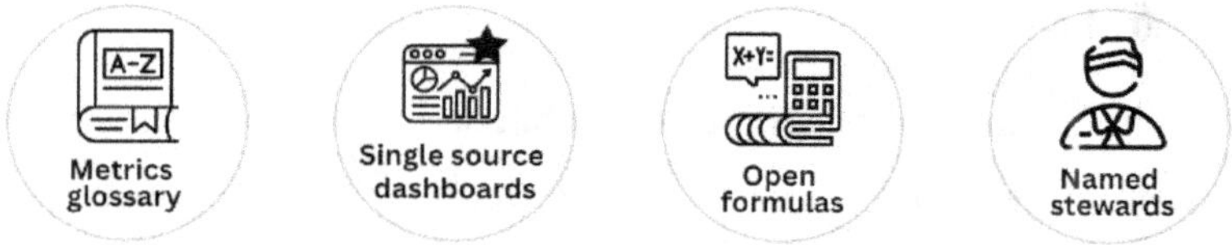

Figure 12: Governance quick wins.

Where shared language gets stuck is in the ambition of the starting point.

Organizations that try to govern everything at once govern nothing.

The instinct to be comprehensive, to build a full data dictionary covering every metric across every function before anyone is allowed to use it, produces a project that takes many months, satisfies nobody, and gets quietly abandoned. Start with the top metrics that matter most. Get those right and expand from there.

The second place it gets stuck is in the ownership of definitions. When two functions have been calculating the same metric differently for two years, agreeing on one definition means one of them has to concede. That conversation is uncomfortable and requires someone with sufficient authority to make the call. This is where the named steward earns their role, not as a technical function, but as the person who holds the agreed definition and defends it when someone tries to revert to their own version.

What changes

The most immediate signal that shared language is working is what happens in meetings. When a metric appears on screen and nobody questions which version it is, something important has shifted. The conversation moves directly to interpretation and decision. That transition from debating the number to debating what to do about it is the clearest behavioral signal that shared language is in place.

You also see it in how new metrics get created. In organizations without shared languages, a new metric tends to emerge organically: an analyst builds something for one stakeholder, it gets shared and adopted informally, and six months later, it appears in three dashboards with three slightly different calculations. In organizations with shared language in place, a new metric goes through a simple process: definition agreed, formula documented, source named, steward assigned. It takes an extra day, but it prevents two years of confusion.

At the retailer, the metrics glossary eventually expanded from eight metrics to 23 over the following year, not because someone mandated it, but because the quarterly review had become so noticeably more productive that other teams started asking to have their metrics included. Shared language had made the ownership from the previous lever real. People were willing to own outcomes they could trust, but reluctant to own those they couldn't.

Ownership and shared language are not sequential steps; they are interdependent. A named owner who doesn't trust the number they're being asked to own will hedge, qualify, and quietly pass the conversation back to the data team. A metrics glossary without a named owner produces well-defined numbers that nobody feels responsible for. Together, they create the conditions for accountability to be real rather than assigned. What turns them into a working system is the third lever: cadence.

Close the loop

A large multichannel fashion retailer brought me in to look at why their data team's work wasn't translating into trading decisions. They sold across physical stores and online, with buying teams responsible for managing stock across hundreds of product lines and dozens of categories. The numbers were good; the sell-through rate by product category was tracked weekly, clearly owned, and calculated the same way across the business. The foundation was in place and the ownership was assigned. On paper, the accountability system was working.

However, in practice, the formal moment to discuss sell-through happened at the end of each buying season. By then, the markdown decisions had already been made, either on instinct, on experience, or on the commercial director's read of the floor. The data confirmed what had happened, but it had not shaped what anyone decided to do about it while there was still time to act.

I asked the category buyer when she last reviewed the sell-through numbers and whether she changed anything as a result. She thought about it and said, "At the end of last season.... But by then it was already too late to do much." I asked when the next formal review was scheduled. "End of this season, in eight weeks." Eight weeks is a long time in fashion retail. A product can move from hero to clearance in six. The ownership was real, the data was trusted, but the window to act was closing every week, without anyone formally required to review it.

The intervention was simple. A fixed biweekly 30-minute sell-through review with the category buyer, the merchandising lead, and one analyst. Three questions only: "What moved?" "What does it mean for the next four weeks?" and "What is the decision?" No slides prepared in advance, no status update, just looking at the number, the context, and the call. If there was no decision to make, the meeting lasted 15 minutes; if there was, it ran its course.

Within one season, markdown spend had reduced by around 18%. Slow-moving stock was being identified and acted on four to six weeks earlier than before. The decisions themselves had not changed; the buyers were making the same kinds of calls they had always made. The timing had changed, and in fashion retail, timing is most of the job.

One owner, one metric

Cadence is the structured rhythm that makes accountability visible, and it's the answer to a question ownership and shared language cannot answer on their own: "When exactly does the owner show up and account for the metric?"

Without it, accountability exists only in theory, not in practice. The owner knows the metric is theirs, the data is clean and trusted, but the formal moment to explain movement, make a decision, and commit to what happens next only comes around at a quarterly meeting, or worse, whenever someone senior happens to notice the number has moved. In between, the metric drifts, the owner monitors but does not act, and when the review finally arrives, the conversation is a post-mortem rather than a decision.

The practical tool is a Metric Review: a fixed, recurring meeting with one owner, one metric, and three questions: what moved, why, and what is the decision for the next period.

The format matters as much as the frequency. Most performance reviews fail because they make decisions optional: 30 agenda items, 90 minutes, a room full of people there to be informed rather than to decide. The Metric Review is the opposite: fixed in the calendar, protected, and limited to a maximum of 30 minutes. Attendees are the metric owner, the person they answer to for that outcome, and one person from the data team. No slides required, and if there is no decision to make, end early. The owner does not present, but answers to their lead: what moved, why, and what they are committing to do about it before the next review, whether that is a budget reallocation, a process change, or an escalation.

Frequency depends on the metric and the business context. A sell-through rate in fashion retail warrants a biweekly review because the window to act is short. A customer satisfaction score in a B2B business might be warranted monthly. An annual revenue target warrants quarterly. The right cadence is the one that gives the owner enough time to see genuine movement and enough runway to do something about it before the next review.

Where cadence gets stuck is in the calendar. Fixed reviews get canceled when things get busy, and in most companies, things are always busy. The first cancellation is usually fine; the second starts a pattern; by the third, the review exists in the calendar but not in practice, and the owner has quietly learned that showing up with an answer is optional. The fix is to treat the Metric Review like a board meeting: it can be shortened, but it cannot be canceled.[11] If the owner cannot attend, they send a deputy who can answer the three questions. Breaking the rhythm, even once with good reason, signals that accountability is situational.

The second place it gets stuck is in the structure of the meeting itself. Left to their own devices, most teams turn a Metric Review into a reporting session, where the owner walks through what

---

[11] This approach has precedent in how high-performing organizations structure accountability. Amazon's Weekly Business Review operates on exactly this principle: every metric has a named owner expected to explain variances and commit to a response, in a meeting that is fixed, non-negotiable, and attended by senior leadership. When a metric shows only routine variation, the review moves on; it exists for exceptions and decisions, not status updates. See Colin Bryar and Bill Carr, Working Backwards: Insights, Stories, and Secrets from Inside Amazon (St. Martin's Press, 2021).

happened, the room nods, and everyone leaves without a decision. The three-question format exists to prevent exactly that. "What moved?" "Why?" "What is the decision?" The third question is the one that matters, and it is the one most likely to be skipped if the format is not held.

What changes

The clearest signal that cadence is working is the quality of what comes out of the room, not what goes into it. When a Metric Review produces a specific decision, such as reallocate the budget, change the targeting, accelerate the intervention, hold the current course, and review again in two weeks, the cadence is functioning. When it produces a summary of what happened and a vague intention to monitor the situation, it is not.

You also see it in how owners carry the metric between reviews. When cadence is in place, the owner does not wait for the formal meeting to notice that something has moved. They track it between sessions, form a view before they walk into the room, and arrive with a recommendation rather than a report. The review becomes the moment they commit to a decision, not the moment they discover the problem.

At the fashion retailer, within one season of introducing the biweekly sell-through review, markdown spend decreased by approximately 18%. Slow-moving stock was being identified and acted on four to six weeks earlier than before. The decisions themselves had not changed; the buyers were making the same kinds of calls they had always made. The timing had changed, and in fashion retail, timing is most of the job. By the third season, the buyers were requesting the review rather than tolerating it.

Cadence is what closes the loop. Ownership names who is responsible; the shared language ensures they trust the numbers; and cadence creates the moments when they show up and answer for it. When all three are in place, accountability stops being something a company aspires to and becomes something you can observe in how people behave on an ordinary working morning.

Conclusion

Accountability is not blame, it's motion. When ownership, shared language, and cadence are working together, something shifts in how meetings feel. The owner arrives with a view, not just a report. The decision gets made in the room, and everyone leaves knowing what happens next.

It doesn't require a transformation program or a new organizational structure. It requires a name on every metric that matters, a shared language everyone trusts, and a fixed moment where the owner has to show up and answer for it. Those three things, done consistently, change what data is used for - from something that gets reported to something that drives action.

I've seen ownership maps in place, cadence running on schedule, and shared language agreed across functions, and still watched a named owner sit quietly through a meeting where their metric was being discussed, because they didn't feel safe enough to have a view. The structure was there, but the confidence wasn't. That's a different problem, and the tools in this chapter can't solve it. That is one condition that Accountability assumes but cannot create on its own. The levers work when people feel confident enough to engage honestly with what the data is telling them, to commit to a decision, name a direction, and be willing to be wrong in front of people who will remember it. Building that confidence is a different kind of work and it's what the next chapter is for.

CHAPTER 7

Literacy

Every team has one: the person everyone turns to when the dashboards stop making sense. They know where the data comes from, can spot when a metric is being miscalculated, and speak a language that sits somewhere between business and technical, without fully belonging to either. I call them the dashboard whisperer.

I was working with a product team at a global B2B company on their product analytics when I noticed something. They had a solid data infrastructure, a clean analytics stack, and a biweekly product review call in place, during which the team reviewed engagement metrics together. On paper, data was central to how they worked. In practice, most of the product owners in the call didn't know what to do with what they were seeing. Not because they were careless or resistant, but because nobody had ever taught them what a 43% retention rate meant for a B2B product at their stage, or how to read a cohort chart in the context of their specific user behavior, or which three metrics predicted whether a feature was working. They had access to all the data, but they didn't have the knowledge to connect it to the decisions in front of them. That is what cultural lag looks like in many teams. Not hostility to or ignorance of data, just a gap between what exists and what people know how to use. The dashboard whisperer fills that gap reliably until they go on holiday or leave, and then the knowledge walks out with them.

That is when you discover that the rest of the team has been deferring, not deciding.

The underlying problem is not only skill, it's also participation. People do not stay silent in meetings because they cannot read the chart. They stay silent because saying what the chart means creates risk. You can be wrong in a way that everyone remembers. The dashboard whisperer has developed enough fluency to take that risk. Most people around the table have not, and until that changes, the data team will keep doing interpretation work that was never supposed to be theirs.

You saw the most common response to cultural lag in Chapter 1. A financial services company with low dashboard adoption and a genuine concern from leadership. Their solution was a mandatory Tableau training for everyone. Three months later, adoption was exactly where it had started, because the problem was never that people didn't know how to use Tableau. It was that they didn't have the role-specific knowledge to know what to do with what they were being shown. Tool training doesn't touch that.

The real test of literacy is not whether someone can explain a metric in a workshop; it is whether they can challenge a number in a meeting when the room has already started moving in the wrong direction. That is where most literacy programs fail. They teach people how to understand data in private, but not how to use it in public.

Literacy, as the fourth pillar of REAL, starts from a different premise: not "Here is what everyone needs to learn" but "Let's find out where each person is, and build knowledge from there." Three levers make that possible, and unlike the other pillars, they work in sequence. **Assess** maps the real gaps before anything gets built. **Grow** develops capability through targeted, role-specific learning tied to actual work. **Scale** makes fluency self-sustaining across teams and over time.

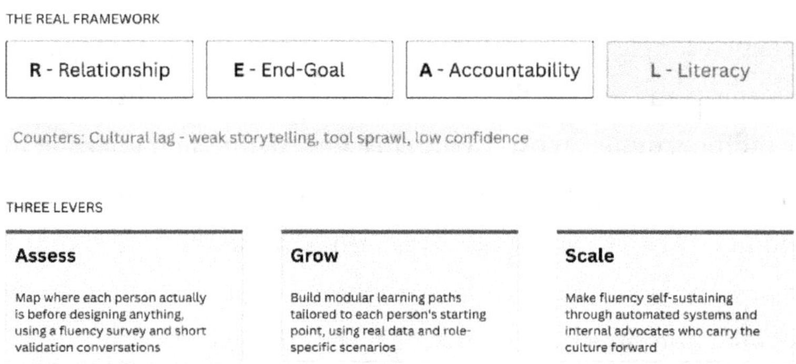

Figure 13: The three levers of the Literacy pillar, with the failure pattern each one addresses.

Meet people where they are

The first instinct when someone says, "We need to improve data literacy," is to start designing the solution. "What modules should we build?" "What tool should we use?" "Who should we bring in to facilitate?" These are reasonable questions, but they are the wrong first questions because they skip the step that determines whether any of it will work: finding out what people know right now.

After identifying the gap at the B2B company, the head of data and I agreed we needed to understand where confidence and capability were breaking down before designing anything. Her instinct was to move straight to solutions. She had already shortlisted two learning platforms and had a rough curriculum in mind for the 60 people across product management. Before we touched any of that, I asked to run a quick assessment first. She agreed, a little reluctantly, because it felt like a delay when she was ready to move.

I kept it simple: a short self-assessment survey sent to all 60 people, asking them to rate their own comfort and capability across a handful of dimensions. "Could they find, define, and interpret the metrics relevant to their role?" "Could they identify when a number looked wrong or was being misused?" "Could they translate data findings into a recommendation?" "Did they feel confident raising a data-based challenge in a meeting?"

What came back surprised her. A third of the group had strong foundational skills and were already doing most of what she wanted the program to produce. Running a basic literacy course for them would have been, at best, a waste of time and, at worst, quietly insulting. Another third had genuine skill gaps; they struggled with interpretation and had limited experience working directly with data. But the largest group had reasonable technical skills and very low confidence. They could read the dashboard, but they didn't trust their own interpretation. Three different groups, three different needs. A curriculum designed for "everyone" would have served none of them well.

Start with the gaps, not the curriculum

An assessment for data literacy doesn't need to be complicated, and it shouldn't feel like a test. The goal is not to grade people or rank them against each other, but to build a map, or a clear picture of where different people and roles sit today, so that whatever comes next is designed for the actual audience rather than an imagined one.

The format I use most often is a short survey, usually 15 to 20 questions, that asks people to rate their comfort and capability across the skills most relevant to their work. The dimensions it covers typically fall into three categories:

- **Technical:** Can they read and interpret the data formats and use the tools they encounter in their role? Do they understand where the numbers come from and what the known limitations are?

- **Practical:** Can they connect data to a decision, identify when something looks wrong, and ask a useful question about an analysis?

- **Behavioral:** Do they feel comfortable engaging with data in high-stakes moments (in meetings, or in front of leadership, when the implication is uncomfortable)? This dimension rarely drives the learning design directly, but it tells you something important about the culture you're working in and how much the program will need to do before it can expect people to apply what they've learned.

Self-assessment has an obvious limitation: people are not always accurate judges of their own capability. I follow the survey with a small number of short validation conversations, 20 minutes with a sample of people from each group, asking them to walk me through how they use data in a typical week. These conversations surface the gap between what people think they can do and what they actually do, and the moments when they quietly stop engaging because they've reached the edge of what they feel equipped to handle.

The output is what I call a fluency map: a view of the team broken down by role and capability level, showing where the real gaps are. It takes about two weeks to build from scratch the first time, and it changes the conversation about literacy entirely, from "What training shall we run?" to "Who needs what, and in what order?"

The fluency map template, the self-assessment survey, and the validation conversation guide are in the Field Guide under the Fluency Assessment and Map.

When assess works,
nobody sits through content they already know.

When assess is working, the literacy program that follows looks nothing like a standard rollout. People with strong existing skills get something different from those starting from scratch. Those who are technically capable but rarely engage with data in high-stakes moments get something different again. The groupings come from the fluency map, not from job titles, because within any given role, the range of capability is usually wider than anyone expected before they looked.

At the B2B company, the fluency map significantly altered the head of data's plan. The third group, with strong existing skills, was redirected into a peer-mentoring structure rather than a formal program. They became internal resources for people who needed support, which benefited both groups. The group with genuine skill gaps received a structured learning path that started with foundations. The confidence-gap group got something different: lighter on technical content, heavier on facilitated practice in realistic scenarios, specifically designed to build the habit of engaging rather than deferring.

Three months in, the weekly product review looked different. Not dramatically or overnight, but noticeably. More people were arriving with a view, not just a question. The dashboard whisperer was still there, but he was no longer the only person in the room willing to say what the numbers meant. The results were clear enough that the head of data was given a mandate to expand the program beyond the product team to the marketing and content functions across multiple markets. That's when the real design challenge began.

Build fluency one step at a time

Assessment is not the work. It only stops you from designing the wrong work. Knowing where people are is only useful if what comes next actually moves them. This is where most literacy efforts, even those that start with an assessment, go wrong: they take the results and design one program anyway, just a slightly better-informed one.

The fluency map from the product team assessment in my example showed three groups with different starting points and needs. The head of data now had a mandate to expand the program to the marketing and content functions across multiple markets, which made the design challenge significantly harder. Three groups across one team is manageable. The same logic applied to 300+ people across different functions, markets, and languages required a more structured approach.

The head of data's initial reaction to my proposal to split the program into different tracks was skeptical. "If I tell my VP we need three different approaches for one team, he'll think I'm overcomplicating it." That's a real constraint. A single program is easier to pitch, schedule, and run. The problem is it doesn't work, and this time there was evidence for that, because the fluency map had just told us exactly why.

The product owner who already had strong technical skills would have spent six sessions on content she'd outgrown years ago. The analyst who could build anything but wouldn't commit to a view in a meeting didn't need more technical knowledge; he needed something that felt closer to practice than training. Running them through the same program in the same room was the kind of efficiency that produces completion certificates and changes nothing.

Before building anything, I drafted learning personas based on four dimensions of data capability: understanding, interpretation, communication, analysis, reasoning. The personas weren't job titles or seniority levels; they were profiles of where someone typically sat across those four dimensions, and what that meant for what they needed next. The assessment results were then refined. The hypothesized profiles were close but not quite right. The real picture was more nuanced in some areas and simpler in others than expected. That refinement mattered because the learning paths were built around the actual personas, not the assumed ones. Building one program for all of them would have been a mistake, so I didn't.

Modular learning paths

Grow is about building data fluency the way any real skill develops - incrementally, through practice, with content specific enough to be immediately useful.[12] The structure that works is modular learning paths designed around each person's starting point and real gaps. The number of stages will vary depending on the organization and the scope of the program. Two people at the same capability level can still need different practical content depending on the work they do.

With the personas shaped by the assessment, I built separate learning paths for each group across marketing and content functions. The formats were deliberately varied: short videos for concepts people could absorb independently, live workshops for the skills that needed practice and discussion, and hands-on exercises built around real data from their actual markets rather than generic examples. The mix mattered. Videos work well for building shared vocabulary and foundational understanding. Workshops are where interpretation and challenge get practiced with other people. Hands-on exercises are where it becomes real, where someone stops learning about data analysis in the abstract and starts working through their own actual results with support.

Here is how the three stages worked in practice:

---

12 The principle that skills develop through progressive stages, from conceptual understanding to critical application in real conditions, is well established in adult learning theory. For more, see David A. Kolb, *Experiential Learning: Experience as the Source of Learning and Development* (Prentice Hall, 1984).

Stage	What it covers	What you can do after	Persona variation
Orientation	Metrics relevant to your context, data sources, tool foundations, and where tools can mislead you.	Find, read, and navigate the data relevant to your role with appropriate skepticism.	Largely consistent across personas. Some personas end here.
Interpretation	Reading data critically, spotting patterns, identifying anomalies, forming a view.	Identify when something looks wrong and form an independent view rather than deferring to others.	Scenarios use domain-specific data and tools.
Application	Connecting data to a recommendation or decision under realistic conditions.	Make a call, own a recommendation, and communicate it clearly.	Exercises must replicate real decisions the person faces.

Figure 14: The three learning stages example: what each covers, what it produces, and how it varies by persona.

The **orientation** gave everyone the same foundation: a shared vocabulary and an honest introduction to how their tools could mislead them. Getting that out in the open early changed how people engaged with everything that followed.

From **interpretation** onwards, the person's actual domain shaped the subject matter while their capability level determined the complexity. In both cases, the data and dashboards were real because sanitized example data teaches people to find the clean answer, and clean answers are rarely what they encounter in practice.

Application was the hardest stage to design and is the one most programs skip. It required realistic scenarios with ambiguity, competing signals, and no clean right answer. The closer the exercise was to someone's actual work, the more the practice transferred. Generic application exercises produce very little change in behavior, precisely because they have nothing to do with the decisions people face.

That specificity is what produces the shift that grow is designed to make. Before, people waited for interpretation: the dashboard exists, the numbers are there, and someone more senior or more technical is asked to explain what they mean. After, people arrive at the meeting having already formed a view. They may be wrong. They expect to be challenged, but they show up with a position rather than a question, and that changes everything about what the meeting can do. None of that shows up in completion rates, which only tell you whether people clicked through the content, not whether anything changed.

When grow works,

capability shows up in the room, not just on a certificate.

When grow is working, you see it in behavior before you see it in any metric. People arrive at meetings with a view already formed, ask sharper questions, and know when to question the tool.

At the B2B company, that behavioral shift became visible within about three months, and it didn't arrive everywhere at once.

Marketing leads across several markets were reporting something similar: content teams were starting to include data in briefs without prompting. They didn't produce a sophisticated analysis, just a more grounded starting point: "Last quarter this format underperformed in this region, so we want to try a different approach." That sentence, confidently said in a planning meeting by someone who, six months earlier, would have waited for the data team to tell them what the numbers meant, is what grow is designed to produce.

Make learning stick and spread

But even good learning fades if it has nowhere to live after the sessions end. Building a good curriculum gives people a path, but it doesn't keep them moving once the formal learning ends. Most literacy efforts have a half-life. Completion rates are highest in the first month, engagement drops off in the second, and by the third month, the platform runs in the background while people do something else. The learning happened but the habit didn't form.

Scale is the lever that addresses this, and it works on two levels. The first is making the capability-building self-sustaining: designed so that it runs, updates, and reaches new people without the data team having to manually push it forward every cycle. The second is building the social infrastructure around learning - the community, the internal advocates, the informal channels where fluency gets practiced and reinforced long after the last module is complete. Both matter. A program that invests only in the first produces good content that nobody talks about. One that invests only in the second produces enthusiasm without substance.

Build it so it runs without you

Making the system self-sustaining requires answering five questions that most organizations never ask when launching a learning program. Who owns it after launch? Not who approved it or who the executive sponsor was, but who is responsible for it still running twelve months from now? How often is the content reviewed, and by whom? What happens when a tool is updated and a module becomes wrong? How do new joiners enter the learning paths, and who shows them in? And what metric tells you the program is alive rather than just open in a browser tab? Completion rates are the wrong answer to that last question. The right answer looks more like: Are people arriving at meetings with a view they didn't have six months ago? Is the community channel still generating questions, or has it gone quiet?

Find the internal advocates and give them something to do

What makes the system run is other people. In every organization, there are individuals who are genuinely curious about data, who enjoy helping a colleague work through a chart, who will answer a question in a shared channel because it interests them rather than because it is their job. These people exist at every level and in every function, and they are the engine. Find them early. Give them visibility, a channel to run, a session to host, a mandate to flag when something in the curriculum is out of date. A community built around them can shift the culture faster than a curriculum delivered to people who weren't ready for it.

Onboarding is usually where this breaks down first. New joiners land in a team without knowing the learning paths exist, nobody introduces them, and six months later, they are doing what everyone else did before the program: waiting for someone else to interpret. Building new joiners into the system from day one, through their team lead or a community buddy, is one of the highest-leverage things a literacy program can do. This is also where the curriculum stays alive. The data team keeps the formal content up to date. The community surfaces what needs updating: the module on the attribution tool whose default settings changed last quarter, and the section on a metric the business has since redefined. Formal and informal work together, and the curriculum stops feeling like something that was launched once and is slowly going stale. [13]

Scale works when the community outlives the one who built it

At the B2B company, the clearest signal came about eighteen months in, when the data team had stopped being the primary driver of the learning effort - new joiners were being onboarded

---

[13] Wenger calls this a "Community of practice", an informal network where learning happens through participation rather than instruction, and where shared knowledge becomes part of the group's culture rather than a one-time training event. It is exactly the infrastructure described here. For more on this see Etienne Wenger, *Communities of Practice: Learning, Meaning, and Identity* (Cambridge University Press, 1998).

into the learning paths by their team leads, the internal advocates were running their own sessions, and when a tool updated and a module became outdated, someone from the community flagged it first. The literacy system had developed a life of its own. If it still depends on one person pushing it forward every cycle, it hasn't scaled, just survived.

Conclusion

Cultural lag persists in most companies, not because people don't want to use data, but because no one has created the conditions that make using it feel natural and worth the effort. The default is a one-size-fits-all training that treats everyone the same, assumes the gap is uniform, and measures success by completion rates rather than by whether anything changed. Most of the time, nothing does.

Literacy breaks that cycle by starting from a different question. Not "What do we need to teach people?" but "Where are people actually starting from, and what do they specifically need to move forward?" That shift sounds small, but it changes everything downstream: what gets built, who it's built for, and whether it lasts.

Without Literacy, every other pillar depends on a few brave translators. Relationship gets data into the room. End-goal gives it a decision to answer. Accountability gives it a named owner. But if the only people who can interpret what the data mean are on the data team, none of that is enough. The marketing director still defers. The product lead still waits. The meeting still ends without anyone in the room having used the analysis to change their mind. Literacy makes the other three pillars possible for everyone, not just those who already speak the language.

Literacy is not knowing where to click. It is having the confidence to say, "I think this number means we need to change course" while others are listening.

What's next

If Parts I and II have done their job, you already have what you need. You understand where data culture breaks down, you have a framework for fixing it, and you know which levers to reach for. You could close the book here and start tomorrow morning with a different set of questions.

The next part exists because at some point in almost every engagement, someone has said, "I get it, but can you show me what exactly that looks like?" So the next part shows it on paper - a collection of tools I've built, tested, revised after they didn't quite work, and kept using once they did. Seven in total: a diagnostic, two workshops, two briefs, and two maps. Everything referenced across the four framework chapters lives here, in one place.

Start with the REAL Diagnostic if you're not sure which pillar deserves your attention first. It takes about 10 minutes and points you directly to the chapter most relevant to your situation right now. If you already know which pillar is most broken, skip the diagnostic and go straight to the relevant tool; each one opens with a short explanation of what it's for and when to use it.

One thing worth saying clearly about how these tools are meant to be used: they're designed to be adapted, not followed to the letter. The questions, the formats, and the facilitation sequences are all starting points. A team of six in a single room will run the clarity workshop differently than a distributed team of twenty across time zones, and both are fine. What matters is that the conversation happens, not that it follows the exact sequence written here. Most of these are facilitated sessions, which means they need someone willing to hold the process, keep the group honest, and ask the uncomfortable question when the conversation drifts toward comfortable vagueness. That person doesn't need to be the most senior in the room; they need to understand what the tool is trying to produce and refuse to let the group skip the question that makes everyone go quiet.

Each tool ends with something you can point to. Those outputs matter. A shared artifact is what makes the common ground you built in the room durable. Without it, what felt like alignment on one day tends to dissolve by the next.

Use what fits. Adapt what almost fits. Ignore the rest.

PART III

Field Guide - Applying REAL in Practice

Understanding the framework is only the beginning. Lasting change happens when ideas become habits.

This Field Guide translates the REAL Framework into practical tools you can use immediately with your own teams. Each workshop, template, and diagnostic has been developed through real client work, refined through experience, and designed to solve a specific problem you've already encountered in this book.

You don't need to use every tool. Start with the challenge you're facing today, adapt the exercises to your own context, and build from there. The aim isn't to follow a methodology perfectly. It's to create better conversations, better decisions, and ultimately, to get data out of the dashboard and into the room where decisions get made.

If Part I showed you why data initiatives stall, and Part II showed you how REAL fixes the pattern, this Field Guide shows you what to do next. Each tool stands on its own: you can start anywhere, skip what doesn't apply, and come back when you need it. If you're not sure where to begin, the REAL Diagnostic at the start of this section will point you in the right direction.

If you recognize the problem, go straight to the tool.

Problem	Tool
You're not sure where data culture is breaking down.	**REAL Diagnostic**
Teams argue about what success means before anything is built.	**Clarity Workshop**
Analysis gets built without a clear decision behind it.	**Decision Backward Brief**
Dashboards get built but nobody uses them.	**Dashboard Design Workshop**
Insights land but nothing changes.	**Action Brief**
Nobody owns what happens when a metric moves.	**Ownership Map**
Training gets run but behavior doesn't change.	**Fluency Assessment and Map**

If more than one row applies, start with the REAL Diagnostic. It will tell you which problem is loudest.

CHAPTER 8

REAL Diagnostic

The REAL Diagnostic is useful when your organization knows something is broken but can't agree on what, or when you're advising a new team and need a fast, credible read of the situation before recommending where to start.

The four pillars of REAL address four different problems. In most organizations, all four are present to some degree, but they're rarely equally urgent. This diagnostic cuts through that. It won't tell you how mature your data culture is, but it will tell you where the pain is loudest right now and which pillar to start with.

16 questions. About 10 minutes. Honest answers only.

For each statement below, rate your organization on a scale of 1 to 4.

1 = Rarely or never - not a pattern we recognize.

2 = Occasionally - happens but not reliably.

3 = Often - more the rule than the exception.

4 = Always - this is just how we work.

If you genuinely don't know whether something happens, score it 2, and then flag it. A question you can't answer about your own organization is worth investigating.

Getting involved

1. By the time data gets involved, the strategy is set, and the decisions are made.

2. Campaigns or launches go live without anyone thinking about measurement.

3. Data gets requested for presentations at the last minute, with no time to make sense of it.

4. The dashboards get requested and built, but no one is really using them for decision making.

Making decisions

5. Dashboards have dozens of metrics and it's still not clear what question they're answering.

6. Analysis and/or insights get presented but nobody knows what to do with the information.

7. Everyone gets the same dashboard regardless of what they need to decide.

8. Requests come in for dashboards and reports without anyone specifying what decision they're supposed to support.

Following through

9. When a metric moves, it's unclear who can explain why or do something about it.

10. The same metric means different things depending on who's in the room, and meetings get derailed debating which number is right.

11. By the time performance gets reviewed, the window to act has already closed.

12. Decisions get made in the meeting, but no one owns them, and nothing changes before the next one.

Data fluency and upskilling

13. People use numbers they don't fully understand (where they come from, how they're calculated, what they can't tell you).

14. Training gets rolled out to everyone the same way, but the behavior doesn't change.

15. Data gets referenced more after a training push, then gradually fades back to where it was.

16. When people have a data question, there's nowhere informal to turn. It goes into a ticket queue or doesn't get asked at all.

Your scores

Sections	Score	Max
Getting involved		/16
Making decisions		/16
Following through		/16
Data fluency and upskilling		/16

A score of 4 on any single statement warrants attention, regardless of the section total. One consistently true symptom is often more useful than the overall number.

Where to go next

Highest score in	Go to
Getting involved	Chapter 4
Making decisions	Chapter 5
Following through	Chapter 6
Data fluency and upskilling	Chapter 7
Scores close across all sections	Start with Chapter 4

Start with Relationship if data is routinely brought in late. Otherwise, start with the problem causing the most visible pain.

Running this with a team

This diagnostic is designed to be completed individually. However, if the topic is already on your team's table, running it across a group and comparing scores can be surprisingly revealing. Different functions, seniority levels, and roles often perceive the same organization very differently. The statements with the widest spread between scores are usually the conversations worth having first.

Chapter 9

The Clarity Workshop

Pillar: R - Relationship | Chapter 4

The Clarity Workshop is useful when teams are about to build a dashboard, launch an initiative, or set up a measurement framework, and nobody has yet sat in a room and agreed on what success means.

Most teams assume they're aligned on this, but they usually aren't. The goals exist somewhere, but they've never been made explicit, compared across functions, or tested against the data needed to track them. Arguments about whose numbers are right almost always trace back to a conversation that never happened before anyone built anything.

The clarity workshop is that conversation. It brings the relevant teams together before any analysis begins, guides the group through five questions, and ends with a goal tree: one shared reference point for every review, retrospective, and conversation about whether the work is going in the right direction.

If your initiative is already underway, the workshop is still worth running. Misalignment caught halfway through is better than misalignment discovered at the end.

Who should be involved? All teams with a stake in the outcome. Aim for people who can commit on behalf of their function, not just represent it. If someone needs to check back with their manager before agreeing to a definition, the workshop will produce a document rather than an agreement.

Time required? 90 minutes for a focused initiative, and up to half a day for a complex program with multiple workstreams. The more functions in the room, the more time some questions will need because that's where the real negotiation happens.

Facilitator? Ideally, someone from the data team; they're best placed to ask the questions that connect ambitions to measurability. However, the facilitator should not also be a participant. Their job is to hold the process, not advocate for a particular outcome.

Before the workshop

Send participants one question in advance, not to answer formally, but to arrive having thought about it:

What is this initiative trying to achieve, in your own words?

The answer doesn't need to be right. The point is that people walk in having already noticed whether their answer matches what they think their colleagues would say. That awareness alone tends to make the first part of the workshop move faster and go deeper.

Prepare a shared workspace: a whiteboard, a Mural board, or a shared document, where each team can write their proposed goals simultaneously before any discussion begins. Visible, parallel input before open discussion reduces the tendency for early speakers to anchor the whole conversation.

The workshop

Question 1: What are we trying to achieve?

Ask each team to write their answer in one sentence. Get everything on the wall first, and only then start discussing. First, ask each team to briefly present their answer before opening it up to the group. Once everyone has been heard, look for the overlaps and the gaps. Where are teams describing the same goal in different language? Where are they describing genuinely different goals that will need to be reconciled? This is often where the most important discovery happens. Teams that have been working together for months sometimes find they've been operating under fundamentally different assumptions about the initiative's purpose. Better to find that now.

Question 2: What does success look like and how will we know when we've achieved it?

Move from goals to outcomes. For each goal on the wall, ask, "What would you see in the world if this worked?" "What changes, and by how much?"

Question 3: Can we quantify it?

Can we quantify it? Is this measurable at all, and if yes, what metric would make you act? Push past the obvious answer here, because there's a trap worth naming: activity metrics are almost always easier to track than outcome metrics, and almost always less useful. The group should be explicit about which type each proposed metric is, because a threshold on the wrong thing is just a more precise way of measuring nothing.

Question 4: Do we have the data and can we trust it?

For each proposed metric, ask "Where does the data come from, how reliable is it, and how often does it update?" A metric that sounds right but sits on top of unreliable data, or data that arrives two weeks after the decision point, isn't useful. Better to know that in the workshop than after the dashboard is built. If the data doesn't exist or can't be trusted, name that now and decide whether to find a proxy or rethink the metric.

Question 5: Are we all pulling in the same direction?

Each team puts their proposed metrics on the table, not to compete, but to make visible what everyone is tracking. The group then sorts them into two tiers: overarching goals that belong to the whole initiative, and subgoals that individual teams own in service of those.

The sorting itself is often where the most important conversation happens. Teams discover that what one function treats as the primary goal, another treats as a supporting one. Getting that visible and agreed is exactly what prevents the methodology arguments from happening later. The output of this question is the goal tree.

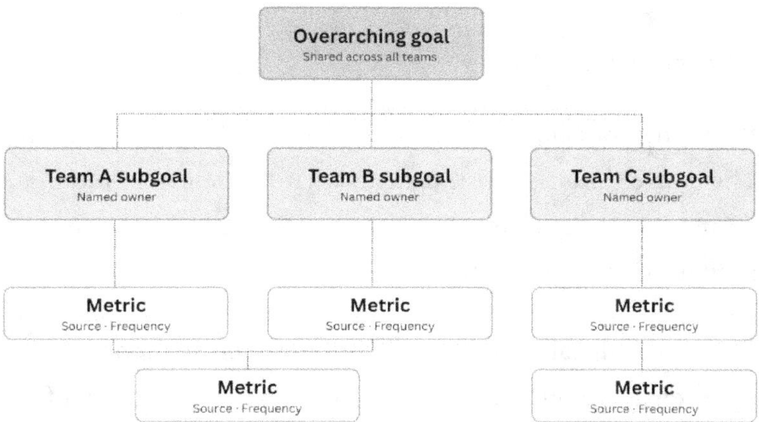

Figure 15: The goal tree (template).

Ideally, you create the goal tree directly in the room, so that everyone has seen it take shape and no one can later claim they didn't agree to it. If the tree is built after the workshop by one person from their notes, it's not the same thing.

After the workshop

Share the goal tree with all participants within 24 hours, as the agreed output. If someone has a material objection, they raise it within 48 hours. After that, it's live.

Revisit it at the midpoint of the initiative. The reality is that goals can shift, data may turn out to be unavailable, and priorities can change. Updating the goal tree should be a deliberate decision made by the group, and not a quiet drift away from what was agreed.

What good looks like

When the workshop worked, you feel it in the first review meeting. The conversation goes straight to what the numbers mean and what to do next, without anyone questioning which number is right or whether the metric is even the right one.

The subtler signal is when people start referring to the goal tree on their own, because it's become the shared language of the initiative. When that happens, the workshop produces something more than a document. It produces alignment, which in most organizations is considerably rarer and more valuable than any dashboard built without it.

CHAPTER 10

The Decision Backward Brief

Pillar: E - End-goal | Chapter 5

The Decision Backward Brief is useful when an analysis request arrives without a stated purpose, or when the stated purpose is vague enough to mean anything. Also, it is the right tool when a recurring report has been running for months and nobody can quite explain what decision it's supposed to support.

"Who should be involved? The stakeholder making the request, and the analyst or data lead who will build it. This can be done completely asynchronously.

Time required? 30 minutes for a first attempt, ten minutes once it becomes routine.

A one-page brief with four agreed answers, completed before any build begins.

Some teams build it directly into their ticketing system so every request starts here. Others use it as a short planning document before the build begins. Either way, the stakeholder making the request fills it in first; the analyst reviews it, refines where needed, and flags anything that needs resolving before work begins.

The four questions

1. **What decision needs to be made, and by when?** Be specific. Name the decision, the deadline, and what changes if the data tells you something unexpected.

2. **Who is making that decision?** A person, not a team. The named individual who will be held to it.

3. **What do we already know?** Existing data, prior analysis, and assumptions worth testing. Prevents three weeks of work confirming what everyone already believed.

4. **What format will help us act on it?** A ranked list, a trend line, a recommendation, a summary. Decide before the build, not after.

CHAPTER 11

The Dashboard Design Workshop

Pillar: E - End-goal | Chapter 5

The Dashboard Design Workshop is useful when a dashboard is about to be built, or rebuilt; the temptation is to start with the data rather than the person who will use it. It is also the right tool when an existing dashboard has low adoption and nobody can quite explain why.

Most dashboards are built from what's available, not from what's needed. The result is a screen full of metrics that nobody acts on. This workshop reverses that process: it starts with the decisions the dashboard needs to support and works backward to what belongs on it.

A structured session is run before any build begins. The output is a design brief grounded in real decisions rather than assumptions, and a clear steer on what to leave out.

Who should be involved? The data lead or analyst facilitating, plus the key people who will use the dashboard, ideally three to five people across different roles. Running it directly with stakeholders is ideal, but not always possible. If the person whose dashboard you're building isn't available, run the session with someone who knows their role well: their direct manager, a close colleague, or someone who has worked alongside them. Second-hand insight is less precise, but still significantly better than building from assumptions alone.

Time required? 60-90 minutes for one role. Half a day for multiple stakeholders.

The four themes

Work through each theme for every stakeholder before moving to the next. The question bank below gives you prompts for each.

Context and environment: Where and when does this person use data, and what does that moment look like?

Current behavior: What do they do today when they don't have the information they need, and when did data last genuinely change what they decided?

Goals and needs: What are they trying to achieve, what slows them down, what would they do differently if the dashboard worked perfectly?

Fear and trust: What would make them ignore it entirely, and what would make them trust a number enough to stake a decision on it? Most teams skip this theme. Most of the useful answers are here.

Question bank

Context and environment

- When do you typically look at data (daily, weekly, or only in specific meetings)?
- Which tools do you use to access data, and how do you find them?
- What device are you usually on when you need this information?
- Are you usually alone or with others when you need to make the decision this supports?

Current behavior

- When you don't have the number you need, what do you do?

- When was the last time you looked at data and changed something as a result?
- What do you usually ask a colleague instead of looking it up yourself?
- Are there numbers you use regularly but aren't fully sure you understand?

Goals and needs

- What's the one question you most often need answered quickly?
- What decision does this dashboard need to support?
- What would you be able to do in the first five minutes of opening it if it worked perfectly?
- What does success look like in your role right now, and how does data connect to that?

Fear and trust

- What would make you stop using this dashboard entirely?
- What would make you trust a number enough to take it into a senior meeting?
- Have you ever acted on data and regretted it? What happened?

Chapter 12

The Action Brief

Pillar: E - End-goal | Chapter 5

The Action Brief is useful when analysis needs to drive a decision at the leadership level, and a deck of findings won't do it.

A one-page document that packages analysis into a format a decision-maker can act on immediately. It leads with a recommendation, not findings. The campaign story and full context are in Chapter 5.

Use it for high-stakes moments: a campaign review, a budget decision, a product launch, a board presentation. Routine reports and exploratory analysis don't need it.

Who should be involved? The analyst or data lead produces it, and the decision-maker receives it. It works only when the data team has been in the room from the start.

Time required? About an hour to produce once the underlying analysis is done. About five minutes to read.

The five components

Situation: One sentence on what is happening and why it matters right now. Not background, not history. Just the single most important thing the reader needs before anything else.

Status: The factual layer, a clear picture of where things stand. KPIs against targets, actual versus planned.

Insights: The two or three findings most relevant to the decision. Not everything the data shows, just the things the decision hinges on.

Action: What to do now. When the data points clearly in one direction, own it, not "the data suggests we might consider" but a direct position. When the picture is genuinely mixed, present two or three options with a clear steer on which looks stronger and why. Either way, the reader should be able to decide after reading this section.

Risk: What could go wrong, or what the data doesn't yet tell us. Not a disclaimer, a signal that the person who wrote this thought carefully enough about the recommendation to anticipate the challenge to it.

Blank template

Situation
Status
Insights
Action
Risk

Chapter 13

The Ownership Map

Pillar: A - Accountability | Chapter 6

The Ownership Map is useful when a metric moves and it's unclear whose job it is to respond, or when performance has been declining, and the honest answer is that nobody feels responsible for fixing it.

A simple document that names one person per key metric, defines the threshold that triggers action, and specifies who needs to know and when. The CPG story and full context are in Chapter 6.

Who should be involved? The people who touch each metric, across functions if needed. Someone with enough authority to make the call when two functions both claim a metric belongs to the other.

Time required? About 20 minutes per metric. Budget half a day to cover a full leadership dashboard. The harder conversation is usually what ownership means in practice, not the mapping itself.

The three questions

For each key metric, work through these three questions with the relevant stakeholders:

1. **Who owns this outcome?** This is the person who will explain why the metric moved and lead the response when it does. One named person, not a team, not a role, not a shared inbox.

2. **What does movement in this metric require in terms of action?** What specifically would the owner do if this metric declined significantly? If nobody can answer this, the metric may not be worth owning.

3. **What counts as significant movement, who needs to know, and when?** Define the threshold that triggers action; not every fluctuation warrants a response, but everyone should agree in advance on what does. Then name the specific people whose work is affected by the movement beyond that threshold, and the timeframe in which they need to know.

Metric	Owner	What movement requires	Who to inform	Escalation threshold	Review frequency

Figure 16: Ownership map blank template.

A note on shared metrics

The most common objection is that a metric crosses a functional boundary, so ownership must be shared. It doesn't. Influence can be shared (multiple teams may affect the number), but accountability cannot. The ownership map names the person who is responsible for the conversation when the metric moves, not the only person who can affect it. If two functions are genuinely in dispute about who owns a metric, that dispute needs to be resolved by someone with authority over both. The map is the mechanism that forces that conversation to happen.

CHAPTER 14

The Fluency Assessment and Map

Pillar: L - Literacy | Chapter 7

The Fluency Assessment and Map is useful when you're about to commission a data literacy program and don't yet know who needs what or when training has been run before, and behavior hasn't changed.

The default is to design for an imagined average: one program, rolled out to everyone, calibrated for nobody in particular. The fluency assessment fixes that. It maps where people are before anything gets built. The output is a fluency map: a view of the team by role and capability level that shifts the question from "What training shall we run?" to "Who needs what, and in what order?" The full context and the B2B company story are in Chapter 7.

Who should be involved? The data lead or the learning program owner runs it. All team members complete the self-assessment. Team leads do a brief validation afterward to flag significant mismatches.

Time required? Two weeks to build the full fluency map from scratch: one week for the survey, one week for calibration and analysis. The self-assessment takes each participant 10-15 minutes.

A note on confidentiality and personas

Run the survey as confidential rather than fully anonymous. Individual scores are visible only to the person designing the program and are never shared with managers or used in performance conversations. Results are then aggregated into personas before being used for program design, so no individual profile is visible in the output.

Fully anonymous surveys create a practical problem: if you don't know who answered what, you can't identify which people to invite for validation conversations. With confidential results, you can see that a cluster of people in content roles have strong technical scores but low behavioral engagement, and recruit a few volunteers from that group to explore what's driving it, without ever sharing their individual scores. Be explicit about this when you send the survey. If people don't trust that their answers are safe, they won't answer honestly, and the map will be wrong.

Part 1: The self-assessment survey

Send the survey to all participants and explain the goal: a fluency map that will serve as a basis for the training concept. They shouldn't think it's for grading.

Rate your comfort and capability for each statement:

1 = Not at all comfortable
2 = Slightly comfortable
3 = Fairly comfortable
4 = Very comfortable

Technical: Understanding data and tools

1. I can find and access the data I need for my role without help.
2. I understand where the key metrics I use come from and how they are calculated.
3. I know what the known limitations of the data I work with are, what it can and can't tell me.
4. I understand how the tools and dashboards I use are configured, including where the data comes from and how it's been set up.

5. I notice when a dashboard might be giving me a distorted picture, for example, because of how the date range, filters, or metric definitions have been set up.

Practical: Working with data

6. I know which data matters for the decisions I make, and which doesn't.
7. I notice when a number in a dashboard doesn't add up, for example, when totals don't match, trends contradict each other, or a metric has moved in a way that doesn't make sense given what else I know.
8. I can connect data findings to a decision or a recommendation.
9. I can identify what a piece of analysis is and isn't telling me.
10. I can translate what data shows into a clear next step or recommendation.

Behavioral: Engaging with data in practice

11. I bring data into conversations proactively, not just when someone asks me to.
12. When data contradicts what I or others expected, I say so rather than letting it pass.
13. I engage with data in high-stakes moments - in meetings, in front of leadership, when the answer is unclear.
14. I know who to go to in my organization when I have a data question outside my own expertise.
15. I feel confident sharing a data-backed conclusion with people more senior than me.

Part 2: Validation conversations

After the survey, run short 20-minute conversations with a sample of people from each role group (two or three per group is enough). Ask them to walk you through how they use data in a typical week. These conversations surface what the survey can't: the gap between what people think they can do and what they actually do in practice, and the moments when they quietly stop engaging because they've reached the edge of what they feel equipped to handle. Suggested prompts:

- Walk me through the last time you used data to make a decision or a recommendation.
- What do you do when a number doesn't look right to you?
- Is there a type of analysis or data situation that you tend to avoid or hand off to someone else?

The Fluency Map (template)

The template below shows a simplified individual view useful for getting started. In practice, once you have enough responses, aggregate scores into personas rather than tracking individuals - as the confidentiality note above explains.

Name	Role	Technical score	Practical score	Behavioral score	Overall profile	Recommended path
		/20	/20	/20		
		/20	/20	/20		
		/20	/20	/20		

Persona view, common patterns, and recommended paths:

Persona	Typical score pattern	What it looks like	Recommended path
Strong across all three	High T, P, B	Finds basic training redundant, already applying data confidently	Peer mentoring or advanced application, not a foundation program
Skill gap	Low T and P, higher B	Wants to engage but lacks foundational knowledge and tools	Structured learning path starting from orientation
Confidence gap	Reasonable T and P, low B	Can read the data but won't commit to a view publicly	Facilitated practice in realistic scenarios, lighter on content, heavier on doing
Knowledge gap in context	High T, lower P and B	Technically capable but struggles to connect data to decisions in their specific role	Domain-specific application exercises tied to actual work

T = Technical, P = Practical, B = Behavioral

What comes next

The fluency map tells you where people are. What you build from there, including the learning paths, content formats, and sequencing, is the grow lever, covered in Chapter 7. The map is the starting point, not the program.

Conclusion

I want to tell you about a meeting I wasn't in.

It was a quarterly business review at a media company I'd worked with for about 18 months. By then, the engagement had ended. I wasn't running workshops or facilitating sessions anymore. So I heard about the meeting afterward, from the head of data. She told me the marketing director opened the review by walking the room through campaign performance for the quarter. Not a deck full of observations. Not a retrospective about what had already happened. A recommendation.

Pull back spending on two channels. Double down on a third. Reallocate the difference toward an audience segment that had been underperforming but was starting to show early signals of recovery. She had a point of view. She owned it. And she was ready to defend it.

The CFO challenged one of the numbers. The marketing director explained the methodology calmly, acknowledged where the data was thinner than she would have liked, and stood by the recommendation anyway. The discussion lasted 20 minutes. A decision was made.

When the head of data told me this story, I recognized the feeling in her voice immediately. Not pride exactly. Relief. The relief of watching something finally work the way it was supposed to.

What changed at that company wasn't dramatic. The data team started showing up before campaign briefs were finalized, rather than after. The marketing director went through a short literacy path tied to her actual decisions, not generic BI training. Every key metric had one named owner who understood the formula, the source, and the point at which action was expected. Quarterly reviews followed a fixed structure: three questions, 30 minutes, one decision.

None of this was technically difficult. There was no expensive platform, no reorganization, no breakthrough AI capability. The changes were small, deliberate, and repeated consistently over time.

REAL changes four things: the relationship between data and business teams, the clarity of the question behind every analysis, the ownership of what happens when numbers move, and the confidence of the people in the room when they do. Not from the outside in. From the room up.

When those four things shift, the quarterly review looks different. Analysts stop acting like a ticketing system and start shaping decisions. Managers stop waiting for someone else to interpret the numbers and arrive at their own view. The dashboards you already have start to matter.

This is where data creates value. Not in the dashboard, but in the decision.

Index

www.ingramcontent.com/pod-product-compliance
Lightning Source LLC
LaVergne TN
LVHW022042200926
848481LV00003B/757
* 9 7 9 8 8 9 8 1 6 1 3 6 1 *